For All Things A Season

An essential guide to a peaceful parent/child
relationship

By

B. Bryan Post, PhD, LCSW

For All Things A Season

Library of Congress Control Number 2002096503
ISBN 0-9726830-0-3

First Edition 2003
Printed in Canada

Cover Art by Patty Lack

Published by
M. Brynn Publishing
Oklahoma

Produced by
PPC Books
Redington Shores, FL

Dedicated to the Tree which nurtured my life,

My Mother and Father,

And the Fruit of my own Tree,

Mikalah

Acknowledgements

No thanks are complete without first honoring God, the creator.

I would like to especially thank Laura Slagle for her time and dedication spent on the editing of this project.

Also, my very sincere thanks to the following persons who have all had a great impact on both my personal and professional being: Lawrence G. Anderson, LMSW-ACP, Martha G. Welch, M.D., and Nancy A. Clark, MFT. Thank you.

And a woman who held a babe against her bosom said, Speak to us of Children.

And he said:
Your children are not your children. They are the sons and daughters of Life's longing for itself.
They come through you but not from you,
And though they are with you yet they belong not to you.
You may give them your love but not your thoughts,
For they have their own thoughts.
You may house their bodies but not their souls,
For their souls dwell in the house of tomorrow, which you cannot visit, not even in your dreams.
You may strive to be like them, but seek not to make them like you.
For life goes not backward nor tarries with yesterday.
You are the bows from which your children as living arrows are sent forth.
The archer sees the mark upon the path of the infinite, and He bends you with His might that His arrows may go swift and far.
Let your bending in the Archer's hand be for gladness;
For even as he loves the arrow that flies, so He loves also the bow that is stable.

Khalil Gibran—The Prophet

"Read not to contradict and confute,
nor to believe and take for granted,
nor to find talk and discourse,
but to weigh and consider.
Some books are to be tasted, others to be swallowed,
and some few to be chewed and digested;
that is, some books are to be read only in parts;
others to be read but not curiously,
and some few to be read wholly,
and with diligence and attention."

Francis Bacon, *The Essayes or Counsels, Civill and Morall*

For All Things A Season

The Three-Phase Intervention

Introduction:

Into the New **Millennium**

"And he shall be like a tree planted by the rivers of water, that bringeth forth his fruit in his season; his leaf also shall not wither; and whatsoever he doeth shall prosper." Psalm 1:3.

As we look at the new millennium we see a time of great change. The information highway is already expanding farther than we had ever imagined possible. Televisions and computers are providing substitute relationships for many people. Rather than sitting down to write a letter or even picking up the phone, we just e-mail; or worse, we do not communicate at all. Instead, we just flip on the television or log on to the Internet.

We have begun to communicate through the computer as if it were a real person. In return, our natural form of communication has suffered. If it is not the parent who is obsessed with the computer, it is the child. Our children have begun to spend more and more time alternating between the computer and the television. We do not pull our children away from this in-home, twenty-four-hour-a-day babysitter because we are very busy and do not want to be disturbed. We allow our children to come home from school, snack in front of the television, and then play on the computer for the rest of the afternoon because they are being so quiet and not demanding any of our attention. In exchange for peace and quiet after our busy day, we sacrifice the quality time we should be spending with our children, which is so important to their healthy development.

Our children will not be in our care forever. They are seeds that are planted in the gardens of our lives only for a brief season. The season to tend to our seeds is upon us. If a farmer does not tend to his field, what will it look like when harvest time arrives? Our children are a reflection of how we attend to their needs. Technology is only one aspect of our society that is taking us away from one another, and away from our children, our most vital resource.

Parents are unaware of the many aspects of our technological world that have become threats to our security and safety. The inquiring nature of a child allows him to come into contact with materials that are not only inappropriate to his age, but which can also be detrimental to his emotional functioning. One example of this occurred with the two boys from Littleton, Colorado, involved in the Columbine shooting incident. The boys became obsessed with the Internet and were further encouraged to destructive behavior by horrible cult groups.

Without parental supervision of the Internet, our children are but innocent babes awaiting slaughter. As information becomes more accessible and the boundaries and structure become less, our children gain knowledge they are not emotionally equipped to handle. Such material consists of fanatical cult groups, child and adult pornography, violence, and more. These are elements of our society with which our children should never have to come into contact. As adults we want our children to develop a high enough sense of self worth and value that they will make a conscious decision to avoid such harmful activities as taking drugs, stealing, and killing. However, if we are not around to teach self worth and values, or to monitor our children in their exploration, then we cannot expect growing and curious young minds to avoid such areas.

It is important to understand that the Internet and television are not all negative. There are very educational aspects of both; however, without parental guidance, these seemingly innocent outlets can, in fact, be very dangerous. Therefore, *as parents in the new millennium, we must always be mindful of the banks upon which we are placing our children.*

For All Things A Season was written to provide parents with an understanding of some of the essential aspects of parenting that are readily becoming displaced during the age of information and technology. It is a book that is easy to understand and to incorporate, or possibly to merely reinforce that which is already known.

As parents in the new millennium, we must always be mindful of the banks upon which we are placing our children.

The Season is Now

To every thing there is a season, and a time to every purpose under the heaven —Ecclesiastes 3:7

The season for raising our children is upon us. Today we are busy, and tomorrow we shall be even busier. Finding time during the season is the first step in becoming a more successful parent. We must remember to make the time to love, nurture, and train our most valuable resource. Most of our schedules are as follows: Wake up, drink coffee, get the kids up, eat breakfast, get dressed, brush our teeth, drop the kids off at school, go to work, come home, cook dinner, watch television, say good night, and then go to bed. When do we tend our crop?

In between all of these things we ask how each other's day has been, argue about the television channel, spend frivolous moments engaged in meaningless talk, and scold our children for their misbehaviors and laziness. "Go clean your room," we yell from the living room couch!

If time of season is of essence, and our schedule is so busy already that we hardly have time to clean the house or to take a pleasant walk through the neighborhood, then what will our harvest look like?

The impeccable M. Scott Peck once stated, "The true road to holiness lies through questioning everything." In other words, you must question in order to challenge your belief system, in order to lead to a change in your thinking, and then in your behavior. Herein lies such a book. It is a book that will cause you to question and re-examine what you have heard and learned in the past. Presented here is an invitation. It is an invitation to stop and reflect on the words presented here and to try to gain a full understanding of the principles behind what is written. If you will allow yourself to be open throughout the process of reading this book, and question the thoughts within it until they become clear to you, then I can assure you that once you are finished, you will look at both yourself and your child in a different light.

The true essence of healthy parenting is parental self-awareness. Parental self-awareness is the ability to look at one's self from moment to moment during parent/child interaction and ask one's self, "How am I feeling?" This one ability, above all else, has the potential to be a major catalyst for change in the family system and, ultimately, in your child's behavior.

Just as the parent is the teacher to the developing system of the child, she is equally responsible for creating and maintaining the environment in which the child is learning. In other words, if your child is bouncing off the walls at home, ask yourself first, "How am I feeling, and could his behavior have something to do with the fact that I am very stressed out from work or just had an argument with his father in front of him," before automatically assuming that the child is the cause of his own stress.

The regulatory (stress management) system of a child is much more sensitive than that of an adult. Children will sense feelings three times as strongly as an adult simply because their regulatory systems are young and in the developmental phase; whereas the adult's regulatory system has been functioning for so long at such a continued state, that it has become conditioned to its environment, and therefore, somewhat desensitized to outside input. It is not, however, so insensitive that it no longer responds. It remains open to influence throughout the lifespan, although it is not as easily influenced as the child's and responds more slowly.

Parents are the primary modulators of stress within the home environment. Whether stress is experienced by only one member or by several members, it affects the entire family. Regardless of where the stress originates, the parent is always the party responsible for calming the stress and creating an environment conducive to regulation. An important principle of parenting is recognizing that stress can flow through the parents onto the child. This is the first step in acknowledging a possible cause for the child's behavior. Subsequently, the natural progression for resolution at that time is for the parents to make all efforts to ensure that their own state of stress is not permeating onto that of the child.

On the other hand, stress may originate first within the child. However, it is of ultimate importance to understand that even in this situation, the primary responsibility for regulation remains with the parent. This is necessary for two reasons. First, stress felt by the child also has a direct affect on the parent, and without the acknowledgement of such, the parent is unable to connect with the child on the level of parental responsibility. For example, if a small child is crying from fear and the parent is becoming obviously agitated by the crying, yet making no effort to understand the cause of the crying, the parent will attempt to remove either himself or the child from the situation. This is classically demonstrated in the scenario where a child is put in a "time-out chair" for a period of time as a consequence to his behavior. Second, once the parent is able to embrace the concept of stress and fear as being the causative stimulus to behavior, then the presence of a negative behavior will be a signal to the parent that the child has exceeded his window for stress tolerance. Therefore, the parent is able to intervene in a manner that will restore regulation to the environment, hence understanding and diminishing the behavior. *This form of parenting is what I've come to identify as Family-Centered Regulatory Parenting.*

Family-Centered Regulatory Parenting is a model of parenting based on a theory of behavior called *The Stress Model,* which focuses on the underlying causes of behavior in children. The Stress Model claims as its basis that all undesirable behavior stems from a neurophysiological state of stress (also called *dysregulation*). The presence of fear lies in between stress and behavior. Unexpressed and misunderstood fear is demonstrated through behavior. The parent can foster the environment necessary to calm, or regulate, the neurophysiological state of stress through understanding, being mindful of, and encouraging the expression of fear or the emotions stemming from it, and thus diminishing undesirable behavior.

At this juncture I would like to emphasize a specific point. This particular point is very important to the underlying principles set forth in this book. My point is as follows:

There are only two basic emotions - *Love and Fear.* The most common misperception that has been established in the mental health field is that our natural reaction to a threat is anger. This is wrong. The natural neurophysiological reaction to a perceived threat is a state of fear. First, we experience fear in the event, and dependent on our past experiences and developmental progress, this state moves rapidly into anger and other feeling states. However, the state of anger is secondary to the primary feeling of fear.

Understanding the importance of the previous statement can move a parent from struggling hopelessly with her child on a daily basis to experiencing more confidence and awareness on a regular basis. Our society, as well, has falsely come to accept anger as a primary reaction. This way of thinking has led us into defensive reactions and ultimately, broken relationships. I have heard of adult parents refusing to talk to their own parents for years and years because they were too angry. Whenever the parent has approached their adult child over the years, they have always been met with a wall of perceived hostility and anger. This perception is certainly being socially reinforced; however, for the parent to look beyond the anger to the fear and hurt, could lead to an enormous change in approach and reception. The point is, if I know you are scared, no matter how angry you may seem at that moment, I can be available to you through all of your anger until you can calm back down to your original state, which is fear. However, if I perceive you as angry from the beginning, then I will be less inclined to spend as much time with you and I will stay guarded myself, out of my own fear. This will eventually lead to my failure in being able to identify with you.

Remember, the natural reaction to a threat is fear first, not anger. The longer a child has been exposed to a constant state of fear in his environment, the more rapidly his own fear will escalate into anger.

Preparing the Soil

A s we move forward in this chapter we are going to cover five specific components that I believe every farmer must utilize in the preparing the soil for a productive crop. In other words, these five components are necessities to a parent who strives to harvest a peaceful parent/child relationship. These components are: Acceptance, Understanding, Empathy, Patience, and Love. Just as stated earlier, these components must be learned, understood, and applied in the context of a holistic system. In other words, failing to apply any one of these components is the precursor to failing in all of the others.

Acceptance

Acceptance is vital to a child for various core reasons. We all have a need to be accepted. Being accepted means to belong, to feel a part, to be invited into a group with dominant values and beliefs equal to that which resides deep within ourselves. Whether it is a group of friends, a human race, community, or a family; being accepted is defining our selves.

Acceptance is the unconditional love that lies beneath the essential life-long commitment a parent makes to his child. This level of commitment communicates to the child, "No matter what may happen in life, you are *okay* with me, and for this reason, I accept you as you are." When a child receives this core message from her parental figure, she will carry this as a stepping-stone into all areas throughout the rest of her life. Many children, unfortunately, do not have this deep belief to fall back on during the struggles of life. Rather, such children live with a deep belief that they are inadequate, not accepted, and unable to be valued and loved. What results is a life of constant self-doubt and low self-worth. Such children grow up and become adults who try to find their self-worth in others, always looking to others, or their work, or their money, to define themselves.

Acceptance between parents and children is the unspoken agreement that within their relationship all is okay for now and forever. When difficult times come, as surely they will, this child knows that he can always return to his parent for security and acceptance.

Understanding

To understand is to perceive what is meant, to have knowledge of, or to be sympathetic towards. Most parenting theories fail to teach parents the necessity of understanding. The failure is not in the parents themselves; it is inherent in the teaching. This teaching began with the parent's parents and their parents before them. Along the way in all of the confusion, they were led further astray by misinformed therapists who themselves had received much the same form of parenting.

The problem runs rampant in our society. We have been directed to look outside of ourselves for solutions, but in doing so, we are missing the single greatest solution to almost any situation imaginable, which is understanding. When evaluating their parenting, it is imperative that parents enter into an interpersonal journey of their own responses and reactions before being directed in how to work with their child. Why? In the midst of the journey, when there is no therapist to guide, no compass to direct, the parent must rely on her own internal resources for navigation. She will be forced to rely on her own understanding.

It is often difficult to understand the behavior of a child because we fail to understand our own reactions to him first. Generally, misbehavior, if not interpreted correctly, will lead to a parental feeling of fear, which will give way to guilt or blame, and in some instances, a deeper sense of shame. When this occurs the parent has already stepped out of range for understanding his child. With this in mind, we shall apply and utilize the stress model: Fear, triggered by the child's behavior, is a great indicator of stress within the parental system. The parent must be inwardly-directed in order to understand his emotional state so he will not cause an interlocking of stress interactions with his child. In other words, when a parent has a feeling of fear arising inside of him about his child's behavior, he has failed to understand himself and indirectly, he has failed to understand his child. When this interaction has occurred, then who remains available to calm the child from a place of love? Love and fear do not co-exist. *Perfect love casts out all fear. —1 John 4:18*

The primary key to understanding your child is in your perception of his behavior. We have been so intent on believing that children are angry, that we have failed to see the true emotions driving their behavior. Most often, it is not about anger at all. It is the presence of fear that causes the dysregulation. Since our society does not encourage emotional expression (except the expression of anger), we are vastly out of touch with our deeper feelings - our core feelings of fear, shame, and hurt. In the process of denying these feelings, we quickly transform them to anger.

The greatest example of this comes from my work with adults. Every word presented in this book can be related back to the adult or parent. If we as parents are not in touch with our own emotional states, then our children will be unable to get in touch with theirs. In fact, brain research tells us that the farther along we go in the aging process, the more we rely on our left-brain hemisphere in day-to-day interactions, which results in more and more neglecting of our emotional right-brain hemisphere. In a sense, we move toward more thinking and away from feeling. This is of importance in parenting because the left/right brain hemisphere research applies to everyone, which includes all parents as well. Your child needs right-brain communication more so than left-brain communication.

For example, Steven over-identified with cleanliness. As a child he had been left to occupy himself, generally alone in his room. This began at a very early age. As an adult, Steven had recurring problems with his wife because he became infuriated over the least bit of dirtiness on the floor, violently accusing her of being dirty, stupid, and a slob. Steven was considered to have an obsessive-compulsive personality disorder. His degree of disturbance seemingly bothered everyone but himself. This example does not refer to OCD personality disorder but rather how the perception of behavior even in an adult can lead to magnificent change and insight that correlates to understanding. The following occurred during one poignant session:

Bryan: Steven, when Lisa tracks in leaves on the carpet, how does that make you feel?
Steven: It makes me angry. She can be so messy sometimes - such a slob.
Bryan: How many leaves are there?
Steven: Probably three or four.
Bryan: Wow, four leaves, that's a lot. That must make you really angry! Steven, what might you say to yourself when those leaves are on the floor?
Steven: Now I've got to clean them up.
Bryan: Why?
Steven: Because I can't just leave them on the floor. Someone might come over.
Bryan: What would they think of you?
Steven: They would think I was dirty.
Bryan: How would that make you feel?
Steven: Angry.
Bryan: Besides angry, Steven?
Steven: I don't know, maybe hurt?
Bryan: Man, hurt, huh. That wouldn't be good. Then, looking at that episode again, what might you have been feeling when you saw the leaves on the floor?
Steven: Worried.
Bryan: Deeper.
Steven: Scared.

Bryan: Scared of what?
Steven: Scared of being looked at as dirty.
Bryan: How would that make you feel?
Steven: Angry.
Bryan: Deeper.
Steven: Oh, hurt, probably scared too (Steven begins having insight). It always hurt my feelings when I would be cleaning up my room and my mom would come in and say, "Clean up your room." I would already be cleaning up my room, why would she have to say that?
Bryan: Steven, when things get dirty such as the carpet with the leaves, it causes you stress which leads to hurt and scared feelings. You quickly change these feelings to anger and shame. Then you blame Lisa for something that is really not that major. Three, four, or ten leaves are not enough to justify calling your wife stupid or a slob. Also Steven, others are not going to think you are dirty just because there are leaves on the floor.
Steven: I never really thought about that. (Turning toward Lisa) I'm sorry for saying those mean things to you.

The anger that was driving Steven's behavior was merely a cover for a deeper emotion. With work, Steven was able to gain insight into his immediate angry reactions and start to communicate and become aware of his deeper interpersonal state. Even more so, Lisa was able to understand Steven for the first time and could redirect him in his outbursts toward her; therefore, further assisting him in his own process of self-analysis.

When a child is misbehaving, you must first recognize that she is in a state of stress. Second, you must realize that she is feeling scared. You must perceive fear as the primary opposition to love. And third, you must accept the fact that her emotional state is driving her behavior. In this manner, you will be seeing your child in a different light and this new understanding makes all the difference in your interaction.

Empathy

Empathy is a common term in mental health literature. The father of the empathetic therapy movement, Carl Rogers, was so adept at experiencing the emotional state of another that he formed an entire therapy around it called client-centered therapy. Empathy is defined as the ability to experience and identify with the emotional state of another person. This ability is one of the most important aspects in a healthy relationship between a parent and child.

It is very difficult for us to move from a place of anger at a child if we are not able to empathize and identify with what he may be feeling. The most common misconception in the mental health field is that a child displaying aggressive behavior is angry. The inherent fallacy in such belief leads parents to behave as if they are relating to an angry child, which naturally creates defensive barriers. How long does it take us to give up trying to help someone that will not get over his anger? It does not take very long before we say to ourselves, "He's just an angry person and needs to deal with it on his own." Once we, as parents, begin viewing the child as angry and untrusting we fail to empathize. When we fail to empathize, we fail to understand, and when this happens, as you can imagine, we will be headed way down the wrong track.

Our own personal history and upbringing may get in the way of empathy as well. We have all experienced various traumas of childhood. We need to be careful to empathize with what our child is actually feeling, rather than assuming he is feeling what we felt as children. This attitude essentially stems from an unconscious desire to rescue a child from the pain the parent himself may have felt as a child, or to compensate for something missing in the parent's own interpersonal life. What makes this inherently more difficult is that the longer we live with unresolved traumas in our own lives, the further down inside we bury them, and they become deeply ingrained into our unconscious drives. For example, parents may have a difficult time in being empathetic to a crying child because as children themselves, they were told that expressing feelings, crying, or being angry was not acceptable. This is much more prevalent in our society for all adults than we realize.

So, the task of being empathetic becomes a two-fold experience. One, for the parent to be aware of her own unconscious and past issues; and two, to look beyond seeing her child as angry, but rather as scared, as we discussed earlier. This empathetic connection will make parenting a much more tolerable and mutually satisfying experience.

Patience

Another major component to making your child feel accepted is your ability to be patient. Patience and its practice is yet another very difficult, yet important task for you to comprehend before moving forward in this book.

Just the other evening I went down to the local gym for my evening exercise session. Since it is a small gym my friend and I were the only ones there with the exception of his two-year old son. Many might find it hard to get in a good workout with a small child present but with patience, what would normally seem impossible, became very tolerable and even enjoyable. For instance, my friend Kim was in the midst of a heavy movement exercise when his son walked over for a little conversation. Between the grunts of moving the heavy weights, Kim tried to convince Tucker to wait just a moment until he was finished. Tucker was persistent. Kim had to interrupt his movement and gently guide Tucker over to a bench opposite him and very calmly reinforce to Tucker that he had to give daddy time to finish his exercise before talking. Tucker seemed content with this bit of attention and was very patient in allowing his father to complete his movement.

This exercise in patience is necessary in the daily interaction with a child. Patience is a process that comes from a center of emotional regulation, a sense of calmness and well-being. As a parent, when you are dysregulated, the task of being patient will be infinitely more difficult than when you are regulated. In general, a state of dysregulation is highly incongruent with a state of patience. Once again, we must first take into consideration our own stress that may be unconsciously driving our state of functioning. Second, we must make a concerted effort to be aware of our child's needs at all times and consider what he or she may be feeling at any given time. In doing this we will be putting ourselves in a place of parental self-awareness and awareness of our child's emotional state as well. And remember, we cannot be patient and loving all of the time. When you do fail in the area of patience you can always apologize for raising your voice or striking out, and promise to do better the next time. Later in the book you will find a discussion of a technique I call "The Three Phase Intervention," which will help at times when we are not feeling as patient as we need to be.

Love

"Love Never Fails" 1 Corinthians 13:8

To tie understanding, empathy, and patience all together is the presence of love. Stephen Covey states, "Love, the feeling, is the fruit of love, the action." In other words, love is not something that just occurs or presents itself. It is something that takes effort. A person does not just feel loved because you say you love him. He must feel it through your actions. This may take the form of a hug, smile, or kiss; but it takes some action before love can be experienced.

The practice of taking action to understand, to empathize, and to be patient, is the process of expressing love. Children need this above any-thing else. All else pales in comparison, if a child does not feel loved. It will do your child no good to talk about how much you love her if she does not experience your love through your actions. The practice of love is difficult. Becoming a parent just to have someone to love is the wrong reason to start a family. I have worked with countless parents who went into such child-raising situations without giving honest attention to their desires. In a sense, it fails to become love at all, but rather an attempt to love oneself more, to make oneself feel more lovable, or even to appear to others to be more loving. Have you thought about what you may be trying to work out within yourself by becoming a parent?

Without going into a sixties rendition of "just love," it is imperative for you to realize that whatever your own unconscious longings may be, you will have a lifelong impact on your child's developing system. If you are unaware of your intentions in becoming a parent, or of any unresolved traumas in your life, you are taking the risk of acting out the same potential hurt onto a child that may have been enacted on you. This will have lasting consequences for both you and your child.

Watering Your Garden

"Train up a child in the way he should go; and when he is old, he will not depart from it." Proverbs 22:6.

We must understand that Parenting is difficult! There is no other way to put it, so let me say it again. Parenting is difficult! There are thousands of aspects to childrearing and parenting. There have probably been a million books written on all of the aspects involved. The fact is that in our effort to improve and become more efficient, we complicate matters and get away from the elements of parent/child relationships that serve to water our seeds and grow healthy children. Raising a child in the way he should go does not mean developing every kind of tool or technique available to try to parent a child, but rather to choose pure water, or the values we want to use to nourish our children, and focus on those. And the farmer must rest well, so that he might rise in the morning and tend his garden well.

We have become such a complex "computer-generated" society that we have forgotten the basic aspects of living and nurturing our children. Here are some points that are essential in watering your garden:

Essential Points
1. **Most historical parenting methods are ineffective.**
2. **Parents parent the way they were parented.**
3. **The parent must take responsibility for the child.**
4. **The child is only as healthy as the parent.**
5. **All negative behavior arises from stress.**
6. **There are only two primary emotions - love and fear.**
7. **Learn to listen to behavior rather than control it.**
8. **Discipline begins with the parent.**
9. **The only true change is change within oneself.**
10. **Parents are not perfect.**

Let's discuss the Essential Points in detail:

Point #1: Most of the parenting methods that you have been taught in the past are vastly ineffective. Parenting is difficult. If any parenting book or course tries to convince you otherwise, then believe me, you are going to be wasting a lot of valuable time and money. In today's world, none of us want to waste either. As you read, you must commit to keeping an open mind. Weigh what you have read against what you have learned and give it a try, not just once, but for an extended period of time.

Point #2: This point is perhaps the most difficult point to swallow. To a significant (extremely significant) degree, you parent the way you were parented. The soil upon which you were raised runs strongly through your roots. To understand how this plays out in your own parenting takes mindfulness, patience and diligence. There is nothing to fear. After spending eighteen years or more with the same parents, it is virtually impossible not to be like them in more ways than just in being a parent. When I say that you parent the way you were parented, it simply means that you behave toward your children in much the same way your parents behaved toward you. Most of us never look at this fact because we do not want to think about unpleasant things, or in some cases, we are never aware of anything being wrong because that is just the way we were raised. At this point some of you parents who are aware of your upbringing are saying, "I'm nothing like my parents." Generally speaking you are probably right, but here is the catch. If you work really hard to not be like your parent, then you are more than likely parenting in the exact opposite way they parented you! You will either parent like you were parented, or you will say to yourself, "I didn't like the way my parents raised me; therefore, I'll make sure that I'm nothing like my parents." Once you've made this commitment, then you do the complete opposite of your parents. Essentially you become your parent because you work so hard not to be like them. There is nothing in between. For instance, when you were a child, either your parents were way too strict or far too lenient, never just firm! When your children become parents, they will feel like they need to do the opposite of what you did; hence, the cycle repeats itself. Really think about this point, as it is important to your parenting success.

Point #3: Today's parenting methods have become highly blame-oriented rather than encouraging responsibility. In other words when the child does wrong in this day and time, we are often taught to place the focus on the child or worse yet the behavior. In this manner, we are not teaching responsibility. Most often times we are blaming them for what are very definitely our own

13

shortcomings as parents. If your child does well in school, you will be willing to say to yourself, "My child has done well because I am a good parent." If your child does poorly or misbehaves, you must be willing to say to yourself, "I must correct my child's behavior because I am a good parent."

Responsible parents raise responsible children. We have often been told that in order to raise responsible children, we must give them logical consequences for their screw-ups in a loving way. Putting the responsibility back on the children to make sound decisions, right? Wrong! A parent who is willing to understand the situation and the child's feelings about a bad decision, is going to raise a much more empathetic child. You cannot expect your child to be responsible if you have never been a responsible parent. Children learn by your example.

Point #4: Your child is only as emotionally healthy as you are. Your child will improve only to the extent that you as the parent improve. We are products of an environment that reflects both nature and nurture. Children are products of their biology first and their environment second. To the degree that nature and nurture are integrated and healthily accepted, the two become interchangeable. In other words, your child can only be as healthy as you, the parent, are psychologically and emotionally healthy. In addition, the child can only interact with others in the social environment (school, neighborhood, and playground) in as healthy a fashion as he interacts with you in the home. As the parent, you control all aspects of your child's social and emotional development.

Point #5: I have come to believe that all negative behavior arises from an initial high or low level of stress reaction in the brain. According to Bruce Perry, M.D. this high and low end level of stress is called hyper- or hypo-arousal and it is the brain's response to the stress we all encounter. Small children often lack a sufficient ability to regulate or balance these highs and lows effectively when the stimulation within the environment and inside of them becomes too demanding. Therefore, it is the presence of stress that will initially lead to an emotion, either love or fear, and will then present itself as a behavior. This formula is the basis for the theoretical psycho-emotional model I call the Stress Model. It is through the awareness and understanding of love or fear that we can help to restore balance within the inner workings of our children.

Point #6: There are only two primary emotions: love and fear. All other emotions have their birth from the basis of these two. If something looks beautiful it comes from love, it if it looks ugly it comes from fear. Even the judging of something as ugly comes from fear, because all that truly exists is love. All things that look opposite to love, such as poor behavior, resistance, temper tantrums, lying, stealing, and cheating; even anger, worry, and frustration, are rooted in the emotion of fear. It is through recognizing the fear that we can take a new approach and direction towards calming our children. The only way to overcome fear is through love. We cannot overcome fear through the use of force, coercion, or threat. These only breed more fear. Rather, we must practice the understanding of ourselves, our children, and the world in which we live. We must practice patience, prevention, awareness, and mindfulness of our own parental dialogue.

Point #7: We must learn to listen to behavior rather than to control it. Oftentimes we have been told that behavior must fit into a certain mold. Children have been raised to become what we want them to become rather than what God has chosen for them. When we seek only to control, suppress, or deny a behavior, we are ignoring the very voice of God. Within children resides the spirit to be perfect, to be whole, to be one with the harmony of love; but our insistence that children fit into our mundane and boring boxes is suppressing to this very essence. As parents the best we can do is to listen to the behavior our children are presenting to us and if it arises from fear, we should seek only to soothe it, and if it arises from love then only to encourage it.

Point #8: Discipline begins with mom and dad. An undisciplined parent cannot teach discipline to an undisciplined child. The laws of the universe do not work in this manner. The Bible tells us that a good tree will bear good fruit and vice versa, what it does not say is that the fruit is responsible for the tree that bears it. In order for us to teach effective discipline to our children we must be willing to look into that space within ourselves and listen to our own higher voice of calling. There may be times when it is we who need to stand still and listen rather than asking our child to do so. In this world of chaos, confusion, and disillusionment, it is easy to get tied up in the race of society where there is only an end. It is in the race of life that we must commit ourselves. In this manner, we will reap the rewards of a good and loving harvest only if we sew good and loving seeds.

Point #9: The only change that is true and meaningful is the change that we can make inside ourselves. In reality, there can be no change other than the change within us, because ultimately, it is such a change that brings forth change in others. When we tend and harvest change within ourselves we reap an uprising of wonderful rewards from those around us. Initiating change through our own being allows us to seek first to understand without the fear of not being understood. Being able to understand becomes a natural by-product of one's own understanding of self. This change is remarkable and powerful, because this change naturally springs forth change in others. Changing ourselves brings about the natural change we are seeking in our children.

Point # 10: Another essential part of parenting is to be humble enough to apologize when you make a mistake. As a parent, you are not perfect. However, if you are willing to accept that mistakes are a very beneficial aspect of growth, then you will be able to nurture within yourself and your child a remarkable system for self-acceptance and growth. Being able to apologize for your mistakes, is taking ultimate responsibility for your actions. This is not only necessary in order to create peace and harmony between you and your child, but this, my dear parent, is the work of world healing. Seek only to apologize and work diligently to do better the next time. Work hard to be a better parent, and in the long run, you will reap the rewards and benefits of having a well-behaved, well-regulated, and intelligent child. You must also take time for yourself to regain your energy and breath, and to learn to be patient because parenting is difficult.

Remember these key points, and they will be very useful to you in the future. Parenting is definitely a full-time job.

Gathering Stones Together

In order for families to be close it is essential that they spend time with one another. We often overlook available opportunities to spend valuable time with our children. A time to gather stones indicates a time for all to work together. Let us discuss some of these overlooked moments and the reasons these moments are so valuable.

Chores

The issue of chores has forever been one that is often viewed in a negative light. Oftentimes, children come to view chores as a punishment rather than as a time for working together with the family to contribute and make the family whole. Most children should have some chores to do within the home. Doing chores provides children with a sense of responsibility and cooperation. Not all children can complete chores in the manner that might be expected. For instance, there are some children who seem unable to do even the simplest task. For this child it is not a matter of disrespect, but rather an issue of not having the internal security to feel that he can do the task satisfactorily. Though chores might be a requirement of the day-to-day life in the home, parents should be willing to work alongside their child to get the chore done, when it seems as though the child is struggling.

One positive aspect of chores is that they can create an order to the chaos that can often be found in a home with children. When children know what is expected of them and when it is to be done, then a degree of structure is already established. For instance, when you wake up in the morning, you know that you have to make your bed before breakfast and then you have to make sure that the dishes have been put away and your bag is ready for work. When you return from work, you have to empty the garbage or pick up trash around the house, possibly feed the dog, clean up the dog pen, and then prepare dinner. All chores must be completed before you move on to the next activity. Chores can create structure in a natural way.

Also, doing chores helps develop the ability to work and contribute at a later age without the child feeling that the world automatically owes him something. Gratification is a by-product of discipline. Delaying gratification is considered to be one of the ultimate forms of self-discipline; however, always seeking instant gratification is a sign of poor self-discipline. The adult who, as a child, never had to wait for a single thing and always got what he wanted will not be able to hold down a steady job or to save money for a rainy day because he never learned the value of delayed gratification.

Chores can help teach your child that there are certain things in life that must be attended to before she gets to kick back and have snacks and television. Furthermore, chores teach children that rewards are received after the work is done. For example, the meal must be eaten before dessert is served. We enjoy dessert more after a healthy meal. If we had dessert all day long, it would not taste the same. Often after we eat a good meal, we do not even want dessert because the meal itself has been so rewarding. Children learn the same way!

If time allows, do the chores with your child. We have been brought up believing that chores are an individual requirement. No way! Help with the chores that are required of your child, and this will create another opportunity to spend time together, to communicate, and to train him in the basic requirements of life.

There have been numerous times when I have requested that my daughter clean up her room before she watches a movie or cartoons. During the midst of us cleaning her room, we become so involved in spending time together, picking up the toys, and talking to one another that she completely forgets about the television. Therefore, we clean the room and get to spend even more time together playing with one another after it is done.

Several times throughout the book I will elude to training. Training is defined in many ways. For our purposes, training means to form habits, thoughts, or behaviors by discipline and instruction. To be successful parents and to take responsibility for our children's decisions, we must train our children in what is the best decision to make, how to communicate, how to clean, and so forth. This is what training means. As children, we are trained in school to sit, listen, raise our hands, and then respond when acknowledged. Imagine how far this early teaching influences our day-to-day lives. Once again chores can be a vital, yet often overlooked aspect of successful parenting. Chores create structure, help build responsibility, and develop the value of delayed gratification.

Homework

Homework is another valuable opportunity to spend time with our children. Children spend all day with the stress of school, trying to compete and please the teachers. Then they are sent home with loads of homework. Once again, Dr. Spock was probably one of the first to advocate for schools with no homework or grades. Dr. Martha Welch feels that all children should be home-schooled due to the tremendous stress they are placed under at school and the stress of being away from home all day. Though ideal, this is not possible for most families.

If we take into context the latest brain research, then we know that school can be a stressful time for any child, but for some children school can be overwhelming. When the degree of stress reaches a level of uninterrupted hyper- or hypo-arousal, the child will be unable to sooth the overwhelming fear residing within his system. Imagine being in a place of safety, but feeling scared all day long. This would surface as worry, frustration, impulsivity, or at other times sadness and loneliness. This means that when your child returns home from school, his internal system might be operating at the same level as if he had been frightened all day. He would be quite tense, as you can just imagine! And parents think that school is all fun and learning. By doing homework with your child, not only do you have an opportunity to spend more time with him, but you also instill a strong mechanism for feeling safe, secure, and calm. So when your child comes home from school with a bag full of homework, sit down with him and help complete the homework.

Statistics show that only 53% of 4th graders discuss school at home with their parents, and only 40% of 8th graders do the same. By the time they have made it to 12th grade, only 33% discuss school at home with their parents. Can you believe that an area of such importance is discussed so little with our children? They spend nearly 8 hours of their day in school, and we are so busy that we cannot even talk to them about what they have done or what they have discussed. Even more important is asking them about how their friends are doing, if they have met anyone new, etc.

If homework has been figured into the time schedule, as it should be, then sit down and help them with it. Parents always complain that as their children get older, they feel less and less a part of their lives. This happens when we do not talk to them about school. Spending time doing homework with your child will enable you to keep up-to-date with what she is going through at school, and where she is at academically. It will create an opportunity for the parents to prove to the child that "Yes, we are smart, and even we old people can help with schoolwork!" Sit down at the table, get your pencil and bifocals, and help your child do her homework. If your child has not brought home any homework, then use that free time to create a special project or spend time coloring or just talking. Use all of the free time you can to create a warm and loving environment for your child.

Family Fun

Today's children spend most of the day at school or in childcare. School entails more than just instructional time. It includes time for physical education, creative arts, and socialization. And there is plenty of time for peer interaction. So when your children come home from school, there is no need for them to go running off to play with their friends for the rest of the evening. There is, however, a need for them to be close to their parents and to regain the connection that was lost throughout the day. Many families relegate family fun to vacations or weekends when in fact, fun is the special interaction within a family that should be the spice of family life. A child who can look forward to coming home to a happy, embracing environment is going to be a happy child.

After the chores and homework have been completed, go outside with your child for a nice walk. This will prove to be an important time for discussing the day's events, feelings, worries, etc. with your child. Making the time to relax with your child through playing a game or going for a walk reinforces to both the child and the parent that spending time together, and sometimes just doing nothing, can be enjoyable and relaxing.

For instance, my daughter loves for us to ride through the neighborhood on our bicycles. During our rides I hear some of the most enjoyable things from her, and I get to watch her develop into a young lady. I truly feel that she relishes our time together as well. We see countless children playing in yards or riding their bikes with one another, and not once has she requested to do anything more than what we are doing in that special moment. Not only does this time together say to my daughter that she is special and worthy of my time and attention, but it also says to me that I am a good parent, and it is okay to relax and just enjoy my child.

If you really feel your children must go outside and play, have them stay within earshot and eyesight to make sure that they are playing with children you know. It should not be a problem for you to be nearby while your children are playing. The close proximity of a parent can and will enable the children to feel safe and enjoy their play even more. This is just the opposite of what we have always been told about children needing their space and wanting to play alone with their friends. It has been my experience that any time I am near my daughter while she is playing with friends, I become the center of attention. I am normally asked to join in, chase the kids, or throw a ball.

Do not be afraid to lighten up and play with your children. The first person that your children should play and have fun with is you. As parents we can become so stuffy that it is no wonder that sometimes our children do not want to be around us. I asked a little boy once in the presence of his mother if she ever smiled and played with him. His response was, "Yeah, twice...this year." And he was dead serious!

> ***Remember Parenting Point #2:***
> ***Parents parent the way they were parented.***

Affection

Affection is another vital ingredient in the time we spend with our children. In addition to spending too little time with our children, we spend even less time being affectionate. Less time, less hugs, and less kisses lead to a lot of loneliness, hurt, and fear.

When our children are first born, we want to hold them and kiss them all the time. As they get older, the hugs and kisses become less frequent, and the yelling and negative remarks become constant. As our children get older, we treat them more and more like adults and expect them to behave as such.

It is unfortunate that we do not understand that love can conquer all. We must realize that children feel most safe when in the arms of their parents. How seldom it is that children get to feel this safety. A hug is such a simple gesture to make; yet it conveys so much. For children, a hug tells them that they are good, they are loved, and they are very important. A kiss relays much the same.

Often times while I am sitting in my chair reading a book and my daughter is in her room playing with her dolls, I call her to me and just give her a hug and tell her how much I love her. The expression on her face is worth more than any amount of money. Afterwards she will return to her room, and I will return to my book with both of us feeling worthier; I as a father, and she as a daughter.

Affection is such a simple thing. We sometimes forget that it is in our power to use it. There is no formula for affection other than becoming conscious of the fact that no set amount is enough, and the more you give, the more you will receive. Start out with a hug in the morning, one after school, and then another at bedtime. In between those times, get in as many as possible.

Why do we not give more hugs or show more affection? *It is because we have been taught not to hug too much or that showing affection is a sign of weakness.* For boys, this is probably one of the biggest mistakes that we make. Our boys grow up thinking that real men don't cry, but *it truly is the real man who can cry because he can become strong, compassionate, and more loving.* Therefore, show more affection to your children. Seize the opportunity to spend quality time with them and cherish them while they are young.

Bedtime

One often-overlooked area of spending time with our children is the use of the family bed. The family bed has lost its hold only within our generation. Most baby boomers can recall sharing their bed with siblings.

Gathering Stones Together

Many parents complain that their children have difficulty sleeping at night and often keep them up in the process. One very simple solution is to allow your children into bed with you. The primary reason that children have such a hard time sleeping is because they become anxious near bedtime. As this occurs their bodies become more excited, hence creating an inability to relax.

Unfortunately, most parents are taught that it is important to train their children to sleep alone in their own beds as soon as possible. This information could not be further from the truth. How can insisting that your child sleep in the other room possibly enhance connectedness? It cannot! John Bowlby, the father of attachment theory, proved years ago that the first years of life are very important, not only to future development, but also to future relationships. Being connected and securely attached at an early age is what determines the extent of your early childhood success.

Most parents want to know when their child should start sleeping by herself. The answer is whenever the child and/or the parents are ready. The important thing is not to sacrifice the connection just to have your child sleep in her own bed. She might not be ready. If this is the case, then rushing her into her own bed will only cause stress, which will lead to less connection.

If you decide your child absolutely may not sleep with you, then you go to his bed instead. Create a gentle and easy bedtime for him by telling stories, reading, or singing a song. Then turn off the light and tell him it is time for bed. Lie in bed with him until he is asleep, and then you may leave. Make sure he has proper lighting because, undoubtedly, he will wake up during the night and come to your bed. At this point if you will walk him back to his bed and soothe him back to sleep, you will ensure that he is not fully aroused in the middle of the night. Do not create anxiety about him waking up. Just lead him back to his own bed. After a couple of times of waking up in the middle of the night and you calmly soothing him back to sleep, your child will eventually be able to sleep through the night.

Bedtime is only a matter of helping your child become more relaxed about sleeping and enabling everybody to have a good night's rest.

Hoeing the Rows

The primary work of world peace is
creating peace in the home... a safe place
for children... comfort...creating a zone
of peace...this is primary work. —Christiane Northrup

E very day we hustle from one place to another, from the moment we rise in the morning until we lie down in bed at night. It is no wonder that we are constantly complaining about not having enough hours in the day to get everything done. This could be the biggest complaint among parents today. You may ask yourself, " How am I supposed to spend all of this time with my child, when half of the time, I don't even know where the time goes." Well, this is where we begin to discuss hoeing the rows. A farmer must pay special attention to hoeing straight rows as he is setting up the framework for how he will grow his crop. If his rows are sloppy and disorganized he will have a much harder time tending his crop as it grows. We must also hoe straight rows for our children by being structured and organized. We cannot expect our children to grow within those straight rows, if they do not know up front what our expectations are. And if we do not provide the structure and nurturing within the straight rows, they will search outside the family for direction, and the rows may become crooked.

This is perhaps the most difficult practice for most parents to grasp because it requires so much work on a day-to-day, moment-to-moment basis until it becomes a habit. A good illustration of the advantage of hoeing straight rows is starting a new job. How long does it take to learn the overall routine of a new job? For most people it takes about two weeks, for others about a month; but what causes us to learn the new routine so quickly is that we do it five days a week, eight hours a day, with very little change in the routine.

Most people who have worked in a single job for five, ten, or even fifteen years have most likely done the same thing day in and day out. They have literally become experts at their profession. Even in some cases where they have advanced to a higher position, they are still doing the same job, but looking at it from a slightly different perspective and becoming even more knowledgeable.

My father is a heavy equipment operator. He operates an enormous machine that actually has the capacity to knock down mountains. He has been doing this same job for almost thirty years with very little variation to his overall job responsibilities on a day-to-day basis. Every day looks much the same as the one before. He knows his machine so well that watching him operate it is like watching art in motion. To watch an enormous machine at work, operated seemingly effortlessly by one man, is captivating. I have been told that my father is one of the best in the business when it comes to operating his machine. It has taken lots of time, effort, and repetition for him to attain this level of expertise.

In order to successfully hoe straight rows for our family, we must be willing to put forth the time and effort. Hard work pays off in the long run. You will reap what you sow, and if you are diligent your children will certainly be a bountiful harvest of all of your hard work as a parent.

Structure

Structure is defined as the manner in which things are organized or interrelated, or the way in which we do things on a daily basis that relates to every other aspect of our day. As it relates to parenting, our children's structure is the manner in which we create an organized meaning to their lives by instilling an interrelated system of morals, values, self-esteem, and social responsibility. So often I hear parents complain of having very little structure in their home and how difficult structure is to create. The truth is that all families have structure. It is just that within the interrelatedness of actions, the important elements are not being conveyed.

Structure is part of everyday life. There is structure in some form in everything that we do. Even now, there is some structure to the things that go on in your home. For some this may be structured chaos; but nevertheless, it is a form of structure! I believe that there are two forms of structure, one is chaotic structure, and the other is organized structure.

Chaotic structure is defined as a systematic or daily process of functioning in a disorganized manner. For example, a family that consistently dwells in a cluttered and unclean environment lives by a certain code. Their code is chaotic structure. Over a period of time the children in this home will become conditioned to accept the disarray and messiness. Most children conform quite well in this environment because it most closely models their own view of the world - very big, with a lot going on! The problem is that this is also a very scary view that sometimes leaves children feeling unloved and uncared for. One of the first things I tell a parent is, "If your house is a mess, you can't expect your child to be orderly." Children must live in an environment conducive to growth and learning. A messy house only conveys messiness both inside and out.

Organized structure is defined as a systematic or daily process of functioning in an organized manner. In school, we have learned mostly organized structure. How else could one teacher control twenty or more students in a classroom? The most extreme example of structure is in a prison. Every moment of an inmate's life is accounted for. There is no room for independence or choices. The amazing thing about organized structure and prison settings is that some prisoners, when released, will eventually commit a felony to get behind bars again because they are intimidated by the chaos of the outside world.

Structure is a part of our everyday life. Implementing structure into the home is not difficult; it only takes time and energy. Remember, everything in this book is very simple, but that is what we find so complex. Life is simple, yet difficult. Literally, there is no better tool than the use of structure in the home to teach your child responsibility, self-esteem, and respect.

Start out slow and pick an area of day-to-day life that you would like to work on first. Use that opportunity to reinforce to yourself the power of structure. Structured time can be as little as thirty minutes a day, but in no time at all the entire family will be responding differently. An example of starting out slowly would be to spend thirty minutes right after dinner every evening for the entire family to have an open discussion about one another's needs. At first everyone may rebel, even your spouse. However, remember that they are only reacting to change, which is very natural for people of routine. Be firm, and insist that everyone cooperate in the family time.

Set down a time limit of how long you are willing to commit and really hang tough. Anything less than two weeks is not enough time to create organized structure. You will be responsible for enforcing the time limit, so be strong. After you see the benefits from adding just a small amount of structure, you will be inspired to go for even more. If you work hard and give your family your best effort at implementing structure for the sake of the family and your children, you will be highly rewarded.

> *Structure and routine are vital to creating an orderly environment and enabling both child and parent to remain calm.*

Expectations

Often times neither our children nor our spouses meet our expectations because of one simple mistake. We forget to tell them what we expect! How in the world can we expect something of them when they have no idea what we want from them? It is impossible! We are not mind readers and neither are our children. This is what makes expectations so important in hoeing the rows. Our outcome can only meet our expectation. If we only expect of ourselves that we will hoe part-time, then it is a part-time crop we shall reap. We must have equally high expectations for our crop. If your children do not know what you expect of them, then there is virtually no way that they can meet your expectations.

What is an expectation? An expectation is something that you expect or something that you are looking forward to, usually in a positive way.

A father was expecting to take his daughter out for ice cream after school. She was expected to be home at 3:30 P.M. At 4:00 P.M. she was not home, and he became worried and upset. At 4:15 P.M. his daughter got home after playing with friends. The father was visibly upset, interrogated his daughter as to her whereabouts, and told her how disappointed he was that she did not come home on time. Clearly she had failed to meet his expectation of being home at 3:30 P.M. After some further discussion, he realized that he was at fault for not telling his daughter what he expected. Therefore, they both missed out on ice cream and the special time together. He apologized and took a rain check for another day.

When it comes to our children, we are sometimes disappointed and upset with them because they fail to meet our expectations. If you go into a store full of chinaware without telling your child that you expect him to hold your hand and not touch a single thing, then you are headed for trouble. Often this is what we do to our children. We put them in potentially embarrassing and damaging situations without ever telling them what we expect of them. When our children fail to meet our expectations, we respond by getting upset and hurt and then sometimes rejecting them. This is embarrassing and also very damaging to our children's overall self-image. Without the expression of your expectations and the follow-through support to meet the expectations, it is unlikely that your children will do what you think they should. Most likely they will fail to meet your expectations because they just do not know what you are expecting.

For instance, how did you learn to drive? You learned first by watching and then by having someone teach you very slowly and very patiently. The teacher told you what he expected you to do and then he helped you to do it. If you do not teach your children first by modeling and then by training them very slowly, you are only setting them up for failure. No one, especially children, likes to fail because of a poor self-image.

The other aspect of expectations is that you must set standards for your children to achieve. If we as parents do not expect the absolute best from our children, then who is going to set the standard...society, peers or television? When it comes to your children, you must always be aware that they want to please you and be worthy in your eyes first. Children will work harder to meet their parents' expectations than they will for their teachers' or their friends'. However, if you do not set the expectation for them, they may eventually resort to trying to meet their friends' expectations because they will feel that they are the only ones who give them approval. Children eventually look to their peers for support because, in some form, they get the reward they are seeking by meeting the expectations of others.

I suspect that children will actively seek to please their parents for about ten years, barring no previous trauma, before they start to seek out the primary attention of others. Children, regardless of age, will seek the approval of their parents. But children, unable to please their parents, may become angry and resentful, and then the pleasing becomes secondary. By the time children get to be around thirteen, the peer group becomes much more influential. If the children do not feel successful in meeting the parents' expectations by this time, they may start to look elsewhere for approval. This normally correlates with acting-out behaviors in school or in the community but the acting-out is almost always while in the company of friends.

It is quite simple to set expectations. The important part is to tell your child firmly and calmly what your expectations are. When your child awakens in the morning, it is important to communicate to him your love for him and your confidence in his ability to accomplish what you expect of him each day. Before he goes to school, it is important to communicate to him that you expect for him to behave, do his work, be respectful, and not get sent to the principal's office. Believe it or not, if you do not express your expectations, then your child may not realize that this is what you expect from him.

Pruning the Branches

By this point, you may have noticed that I have made no mention of planting your seeds. Why you may ask? Our children are planted naturally into our lives. Just as for all things there is a season, so too does it apply to parenting and children. What we must remember is that our children do not belong to us. They are placed into our lives for safekeeping. They are planted into the gardens that we tend, whether we tend them mindfully or not. Not only do children have an expectation of greatness beyond us, but often times they are provided to us as a catalyst for our own growth. There is no patience developed like the patience created from being a parent. A farmer prunes away unnecessary branches so that they do not soak up the nutrients intended for a healthy tree. Therefore, we should seek to prepare a well-tended garden, to hone the banks near that great universal river which will provide the basic needs and highest nutrients, and to prune away anything that could harm our children. It is from this place that our children will sprout forth into all that they are meant to be.

Prevention

The practice of prevention seldom exists in this world of intervention. We become so consumed with correcting and suppressing undesirable behavior, that this has become our only focus. Focusing solely on the fruit leads to a forsaking of the soil from which the tree sprouted. If we tend the garden and nurture the seeds today, we will not have to worry about the fruit of tomorrow. So, too, does prevention apply to children and their behavior. When we practice prevention we are making a mindful effort to recognize what our children can and cannot tolerate. From this perspective, we can move forward with them into a place where they can live without overwhelming degrees of stress for extended periods of time. Proper practice of prevention is the essence of discipline. However, prevention is also a fundamental aspect of taking responsibility as opposed to blaming. Focusing on behavior is blame-based, meaning that the child is often times blamed for his behavior. Responsibility is reciprocal and says to the parent that if the child is acting out, the parent has equal responsibility to understand the root cause of the child's behavior.

Parental Responsibility

According to The Stress Model parents are the external teachers to the rapidly developing systems of their children. In order to be a successful teacher you must first be a successful student. By this I mean that in order to convey a sense of calm, warmth, and love to your child, you must feel it first within yourself. Regardless of how calm you appear to be externally, if your brain-body connection is in a state of fear, you are going to convey this fear to your child. As a parent, you must be aware of your own state of internal regulation before you can effectively convey regulation to your child.

> ***Example #1:*** *Jim was a successful father and husband. He and Susan had been married for twelve years and had two children, one five and the other eight. Jim was a level representative for a brokerage firm and his job was very stressful. In the evenings, after a stressful day of work, Jim would arrive home and immediately hug both Susan and the children. He would then proceed into his home office to process his day and calm his tense nerves. Following a half-hour break, Jim would return to his family and enjoy the rest of the evening playing with the children and talking to Susan. Both children were always eager to spend time with their father.*

> ***Example #2:*** *Nathan was a successful car salesman. He had been with his company for eleven years and had been the "salesman of the year" for the last eight years running, a company record. Nathan and Barbara had been married for eight years and they had two children who were four and six. When Nathan would come home from a particularly stressful day he would not say a single word to anyone in the home. He would turn on the television and sit unresponsively for an hour before it was time for dinner. Intermittently, he would yell to the children to settle down or for Barbara to quiet down. During these times, the family home was extremely tense and sad.*

Both of these men were successful in their respective careers; however, it was the difference in their abilities to be aware of their regulatory states that set them apart as successful fathers and husbands. In Jim's awareness of his internal state, he was being a responsible parent by knowing how he was feeling and that his feelings had nothing to do with his family. In doing so, he would take the necessary time to calm down and process his day before he had significant interaction with his family. This allowed him to be emotionally present for both his wife and his children. Nathan, on the other hand, was not as likely or willing to take responsibility for his feelings. Just entering the home after a stressful day at work and not saying a single word sets the regulatory tone for the entire family for the rest of the evening. No matter how far away Nathan's family tried to stay from him physically, the pressure could be felt.

In parenting, it must be understood that the child's brain-body connection is sensitive to stress to begin with. Then, when a parent also brings his own stress into the family scenario, behavioral upset and demonstrations by the child are nearly unavoidable. Therefore, the first major task of the parent is to take responsibility for his own internal state of balance and calm before considering the child as being out of balance on his own accord. Otherwise, confronting the behavior of a child when it is stemming from the stress of a parent is both unfair and damaging. By damaging, I mean that to discipline or intervene with a child for behaviors that are stemming from the stress of the parent, is to blame the child rather than to take responsibility for the presenting situation.

I am not saying, by suggesting that the parent take responsibility, that the parent is to blame. All too often I hear, "It's not my fault." Taking responsibility is not the same as taking the blame. Besides, how could you take the blame for all your child has experienced throughout the day while you were gone? You couldn't. Parents often mistakenly think that their child blames them when she has had a bad day; therefore, she acts angry towards them. This is an error in our thought. The Stress Model assumes that children do not intentionally direct anger toward their parents as some form of obscure projection. The child may have had something go wrong in her day that has evoked a fear reaction. Because the child is unable to calm her own fears, the emotion simmers until it surfaces through her behavior in the form of anger. The child is not blaming the parent. She is only acting out the way she feels, and she needs a parent to take the responsibility in helping her to connect with her feelings so that her internal stress will relax and the behaviors will diminish. Sure, the child may express anger, but to mistake this for her being angry with you is faulty logic.

Parents can take responsibility for their own internal state through various ways:

1. *Self-Talk*: The parent says to himself, "What I am feeling right now is..." "Is there something that I am feeling that could be causing my child to behave in this way?" or "I am feeling stressed out, angry, or sad, right now. I shouldn't take this out on my child."

2. *Expression of Emotions*: The parent says to her spouse or child, " I am feeling really angry or sad," or "I feel angry when you talk to me in that manner."

3. *Rational Processing*: The parent says to himself, "Why is her behavior making me feel so angry, hurt, scared, or sad?" Then he takes this statement and tries to connect it to the core issue that is being triggered through the behavior the child is displaying.

4. *Conscious Awareness*: If a parent is aware of any traumatic events in her child's life, this may be affecting her interactions with her child. Sometimes our children do experience unavoidable or unexpected trauma that may be very troubling to us as parents. If this is the case, the parent should seek individual psychotherapy to help her process the trauma and then begin listening to herself on a moment-to-moment basis for the internal messages received and perceived through relationships with her children.

5. *Individual Therapy*: For a parent who has suffered trauma during his own childhood, individual therapy may very well be a necessity before that parent will be able to effectively move into the range of effectively parenting his own child. The art of individual therapy is to assist the individual in bringing unconscious material into conscious awareness, in order to give the individual an opportunity to process the material appropriately. Just like the other techniques mentioned above, the assistance of a therapist allows the patient a "regulatory" figure with whom he can build a relationship of trust that will be conducive to positive growth.

6. *Marital Therapy*: If individuals are involved in a marriage where one or both have suffered childhood trauma, it is a necessity that they both seek marital therapy. Perhaps only one of the two has suffered trauma. Even so, it is important that the spouse be included in the therapeutic process because he or she will be a necessary change element in the healing of the spouse. Even if neither parent has experienced a traumatic history, marital therapy may still be warranted to help the parent(s) deal with the stress and fear in the family.

Pre-Planning

Pre-Planning is an important discipline-prevention tool because it enables the parent to plan ahead for any unexpected behavior. Furthermore, pre-planning is a way for the parent to take a moment and think, "Now in the past, Billy has not done well after one hour in this situation, so I ought to plan on returning within an hour." You would be amazed to know how many parents are actually attuned enough to their children to know their limits in certain situations. Through pre-planning, parents are taking responsibility for any future occurrences, which may arise.

Mary was concerned about her daughter Sarah's troubling behavior during shopping trips. Each trip would end in Sarah throwing a kicking and screaming tantrum and Mary having to leave the store with her before finishing her shopping. I suggested that Mary take Sarah to Wal-Mart on a few separate occasions to monitor and determine Sarah's limits for shopping. Now Sarah was only four, so the older your child, the longer she can usually last. For example, Mary knew that when she went to the store with Sarah, they could spend an enjoyable half-hour before Sarah would get restless and start to squirm. It was only when the squirming started that trouble would begin. In understanding this about Sarah, Mary would always make a list before shopping and know exactly how long she had before the squirming began. On occasions when Mary had a really long list, she would either leave Sarah at home with her Dad, Bill, or Mary would have Bill come along to look after Sarah in the store. It wasn't very difficult for Mary to learn about and adjust to Sarah's limits for shopping.

Pre-planning not only helps you avoid possible discipline problems, but it will also help you stick to what is on your list when you go shopping. Who does not go into a store and come out with more than what is on the list? Knowing that your child will start a scene if his shopping tolerance limit is tested will give you added incentive to get in and out quickly. It also helps to bring along a favorite book, blanket, or special pillow to make the trip more enjoyable for your child.

Another example of pre-planning is to prepare for a long trip by bringing snacks, games, crayons, coloring books, pillows, and a blanket. This enables the children to stay occupied during the long drive, thereby avoiding unnecessary anger and hurt feelings. Pre-plan for an evening visiting with friends by not allowing your children to nap all day. What is the likelihood they are going to be ready to go to bed at 8:30 P.M. and give you time to visit with your friends if they have slept during the day? It is not going to happen!

Pre-planning is much the same as structure. By lining out the day's activities or the summer's events, you are allowing your children an opportunity to prepare for what is coming up so they do not have unnecessary anxiety, which can lead to whining, clinging, and squirming.

Time-In

Time-In is what I recommend to replace the more common practice of *time-out*. Most often children begin to get out of hand because some stimulus in their environment offsets their physiology and causes a spike in their emotion of fear. Remember, children communicate through their behavior.

When this occurs, the only way to help a child overcome her fear is to help her express it. A low-intensity way of helping your child return to a calm state is time-in. For example, if your children are playing together, and one continues to whine and tattle on the other, then this is a prime indicator that she is in an upset state. Whining indicates a need for something your child cannot communicate. Tattling as well is a need for attention that your child is equally unable to communicate. The best way to handle this is by stating, "I can see that you are in need of something; why don't you come and sit beside me until you feel better." Amazingly your child will sit beside you until she feels calm, or she will say, "That's okay," and effectively solve the problem herself.

Another effective time to use time-in is when your child is around a large group of strangers or other children. All of the external stimulation will surely be physiologically upsetting for your child. By requesting Time-In before she gets scared, you will be practicing prevention of future upset.

The concept of Time-In is essentially the same as time-out; it just does not require the child to sit alone with her upset feelings to figure out her mistakes. Time-In offers a very low-intensity, safe way for your child to feel safe, and calm down to a behaviorally acceptable level. I am often quoted as saying, "Children act out because they need attention, not for attention." In other words, when your child is acting outwardly this is a sign that she has gone beyond her own capacity to calm herself and make herself feel safe, and she needs you to assist her.

The Three-Phase Intervention

"For I am the Lord, Your God, who takes hold of your right hand and says to you, "Do not Fear; I will help you."
—*Isaiah 41:13*

Before we go any further I will now introduce you to the most powerful intervention available in parenting. This tool along with *Time-In* is the only intervention method I utilize because of my strong belief that prevention is of critical importance over intervention. I am going to explain to you why this intervention is so effective. Most parents want tools to utilize with their children. The reason the Three-Phase Intervention is so powerful is because it applies the same principles in the intervention that make up The Stress Model itself. The technique, *Reflect-Relate-Regulate*, looks a lot like *Behavior-Emotions- Stress*. After reading the rationale for the Three-Phase Intervention, you will understand why this technique is so powerful. It is The Stress Model within a parenting intervention.

Phase 1: Reflect – The following story illustrates the effectiveness of this phase. After this illustration and its discussion I will provide you with the clinical assumption as to why this technique was so powerful with this family.

> *Every night there was a battle in the Johnson home. Sharon, the nine-year old daughter, was highly resistant to bathing. Jan, her mother, was dead set on ensuring that her daughter was clean. Put the two of them together and we have a volatile situation every evening before bedtime. When Jan contacted me about the trouble she was having with her daughter, this is what she had to say: "We are having a battle every single night around bath time. It seems like as soon as I mention the word, Sharon goes into an out-of-control rage. We've been through it all. I've recently begun 'holding' her every time she goes into the rage because I've read this is supposed to calm her down. After an hour of fighting, screaming, and kicking she seems to relax somewhat and will go take a bath, but I just can't keep this up every single night. Do you have any suggestions?"*
>
> *After reading Jan's note to me I immediately thought about the three-phase intervention. I felt this would be a prime opportunity to demonstrate its effectiveness to Jan. It is important to interject here that I often do consultations via e-mail to assist parents with specific behavioral difficulties. I eventually went to do intensive work with Jan and Sharon on their trauma histories, but up to this point, our only correspondence had been through e-mail... Here's what I stated to Jan: "The first thing I want you to do is stop any form of intervention holding. It's not appropriate in this situation and most of the time parents aren't in an appropriate emotional state to utilize the technique to begin with. Next, what I want you to do is to follow these three basic steps. It's called the Three-Phase Intervention: Reflect, Relate, and Regulate. As soon as you mention to Sharon that it is time to take a bath, and she goes into her normal reaction of raging and flailing, I want you to do nothing more than sit on the bed patiently, calmly, and quietly - nothing more. As you do this, I want you to reflect on how you feel inside of your stomach and heart. With the feelings in your stomach and heart, relate to the pain that your daughter feels at that moment. She obviously is in pain, is hurting, or is afraid about something*

around bath time. It is your responsibility to calm this feeling inside of her because it is connected to her stress and displayed through her behavior. When you are able to reflect and relate, you will notice that soon afterward the two of you will fall into a natural physiological alignment, and you will both begin to regulate. When that occurs Sharon will either be calm enough to communicate to you about what she is feeling or she will feel okay to go and take her bath because her stress will be adequately regulated. Give it a go and get back with me."

This is what she wrote back to me the next day: "Certainly, after reading that stuff about doing nothing, I couldn't imagine that it would work. We had tried everything before, even 'doing nothing' as is pre-scribed in parenting books. She would just go on with life, not worrying about a bath, and that bothered me much more than it did her. Of course, we were doing the holding as well, which was becoming physically diffi-cult and seemingly not appropriate most of the time, so I thought, 'well why not?' That evening when bath time was approaching, I started to play back everything you had said. I actually began to get anxious just thinking about another blown evening. I mentioned the magic word and wham-o, out came a good one. I think maybe she was saving it just for this particular evening. I sat on the bed and just watched her. Before I could even begin to deeply reflect on my own feelings, she stopped; she got up, crawled onto my lap, seemingly for a hug, seemed to realize that she didn't need one, and went and took her bath! Let me just say that I was nothing short of flabbergasted. I don't know what happened, but in ten seconds we went from having a knock down drag out every night to the first compliant bath in a long, long time."

I have found that the first step in directing parents on parenting and intervening with their child is to have them take a step back, as the parent, and reflect. To reflect means to ponder or meditate. Of course, in the midst of parenting chaos we do not have time to meditate, but we do have time to ponder our internal world. We have to take a step back and think about how we as the parent are feeling or what we may or may not be communicating.

In the past, I used the word relax instead of reflect, but I did not feel that relax was significant enough in the intervention of a parent into their own neurophysiological state of stress, so I changed it to reflect. The word reflect makes one think of Jesus going into the wilderness for forty days and nights. Not only must we reflect constantly throughout the day in our interaction with our children, but we must make certain we also do it in the midst of intervening in their behavioral states.

When the parent stops to reflect on his own internal state, he is doing three important things. First, he is taking responsibility for his own beliefs, attitude, and stress at that moment; second, he is taking responsibility for his child by being aware of himself before blaming his child; and third, he is ensuring responsibility for the environment his child is in at that moment. It is essential that the parent take a step back and think for a moment, "Am I stressed out right now? Is there something that I'm doing that could be causing my child to behave the way that she is behaving? How am I feeling right now?"

Why is this important? It is important because the parent may be feeling overwhelming stress at that moment which may have nothing to do with the child. Small things mount up to huge things, and if the parent is not aware of all these small things mounting up, then eventually the child does something that becomes, "the straw that broke the camel's back!" If the child becomes the straw, then eventually he will be looked at as the source of breaking the back, when in fact, he was just another small weight in the overall load of the parent's life. For instance, we have many things that we are thinking about, and our bodies are escalating to a higher level of stress. All of a sudden, our child pushes his sister, and we say, "I can't believe you did that!" Here comes all the stress that we have been feeling. We put it all on our child because we are not identifying that this really has very little to do with him. My point is, that on another day, when we are feeling calm and completely at peace with ourselves, that behavior from our child would be handled differently - one hundred and eighty degrees differently. We would say, "Oh! Are you okay? What's going on? Come here. Come here and sit on my lap." But this day, because we are so stressed, we immediately jump up and put all of the blame on the child because, not only has he made his little sister cry, but he has just stressed us out, too! All of a sudden he has become this awful child that needs to go to his room and have a time-out. He is bombarded with all of this stress that is coming primarily from us, the parent, in the situation. Because we are emanating all of this stress, we have made the situation even more difficult than it would have been otherwise. Since the first phase of the intervention is the most difficult of all the phases, the following process will help you accomplish your goal:

An excellent way to begin the reflection process can be accomplished in the form of the **Reflection Response**. *Strive for this to become your immediate response to your child's acting out. The importance of this process is in trying to connect with unacknowledged feelings. The first thing to do is* **Recognize the State** *- recognize that you are starting to feel dysregulation within your own body. It may be situational or it may be general tension having built up during the day. Stop and say to yourself, "I'm getting tense," or "I'm getting stressed." Second,* **Activate the Internal System** *–place your right hand over your heart or directly onto* *your stomach. Take three deep breaths and cognitively let your brain communicate to you what is being activated in your right brain. Allow that communication to take place in order for you to acknowledge your feeling state and to put it within your personal power. Third, you must* **Feel, Feel and Process** *- pronounce the feeling for what it is. Say the words out loud. Give life to the energy lurking in your body, trying to take over the situation. Say out loud, "I am feeling like I'm not doing it good enough," or "I feel hurt, sad, scared, ashamed, guilty, confused," or any number of feelings. Continue to state that feeling over and over until you can claim it as within your own power. When this has occurred you will be back in a state that will allow you to effectively intervene with your stress-sensitive child without overwhelming her even more than she already may be.*

Phase 2: Relate – The ability to relate to our children is a very special and unique quality. To relate means to understand, to get to know, to accept. If I really want to be close to you I need to be able to relate to you. Relating to our children is a very difficult thing for parents to do. We do not want to get to know our children. Instead, we want our children to do as we say, not to question authority, and not to talk back. All of these are very non-relational requests.

Children need a parent to connect with the pain they may be feeling and understand the hidden elements of their lives. If the parent fails to relate to the child, then the parent will fail to establish a healthy and fruitful relationship with the child.

Learning to relate can also be difficult, but it is much more within your parental grasp once you have successfully made it through the Reflection Response process, and you are in a natural place for child correction. In order to help you better grasp the principal of relating, I have created a three-step process for this as well, called the *Relating Reaction*.

To begin the **Relating Reaction***, you must* **Acknowledge the State** *- pronounce out loud to your child, "I see you," " I hear you," or "I'm feeling you." This will allow your child to realize, possibly for the first time, that she is being seen, heard, or felt. I once had a mother that e-mailed me about her daughter. She had snippedly nicknamed her "Talkative Tina." I asked the mother if she ever listened to her daughter. She replied, "Well actually, I stopped doing that about six months ago when my life started to lose its meaning!" When a child cannot feel seen, heard, or felt, then she will naturally go into a state of stress. When there is no connection for a significant time, the body will go into panic. In this case, lack of communication triggered increased*

37

stress, which resulted in a very talkative child. Second, you must **Identify the State** - send the signal to your child of your own emotional state by saying, "I feel sad, hurt, or embarrassed. I wonder if you might be feeling any of these things. Maybe you are angry." Make the statement as a way of signaling that you understand, rather than as a way of needing the child to communicate the feeling to you. It is often difficult for a child to identify his own feeling state anyway. Pressure to get your child to communicate his own state may only elevate his already existing level of stress. If pressured, he might believe that if he cannot give you the right feeling, then you may get rid of him or punish him. Avoid at all cost, anything that might elevate the child's stress to a higher level. The third step is to **Support the State** - once you have acknowledged and identified the state, one of two things is likely to happen. Either your child will naturally calm down and move into the step of regulation automatically, or she will continue to remain in the state of dysregulation. If your child moves into a state of regulation, then naturally things have progressed evenly with minimal disruption. If your child's stress stays activated, then pronounce to your child, "I can see that you are stressed which is causing you to feel really hurt, scared, or angry. I'm going to stay here with you until we can help you to calm down." This should occur in the most non-threatening manner possible. I have always said, at the risk of doing something damaging in parenting intervention, do nothing! An example of this is when I instructed Jan to sit on the bed and do nothing. Any state of dysregulation that is unconsciously transmitted to the child is overwhelming enough, but if combined with physical intervention, it can become damaging. In some well-documented cases, the lifelong work of leading pioneers in the mental health field has been obscured due to the inappropriate use of an intervention by an unconsciously driven parent, even leading to the child's death. This step of supporting the state is serious. If you have not addressed your own stress during the Reflection Response phase, then you literally have no business attempting to correct your child. In this manner, it becomes control and there is no place for control in parenting. To reinforce this particular point, I had a mother commence to tell me that she had to physically restrain her child during times of activation because he would hit and kick her during his rage. She stated that he would immediately go after her when angry. I pondered the statement for a moment and asked, "Do you ever try to grab him when he's really angry?" She replied, "Well of course, I've got to try to control his behavior." I responded, "Well then be prepared to be hit because when he is in the most frightened state and you make quick movements to CONTROL him, you are caus-

ing a fear-based reaction in him. It's the age-old fight or flight re-sponse!" At that moment the light bulb seemed to flash on for her.

Phase 3 – Regulate - The natural outcome following the phases of reflecting and relating is the state of regulation. If you can imagine a cyclist pumping hard up a hill, a very steep hill, and as he gets closer to the top he attempts to pick up speed, but the muscular output for the task has doubled. Internally, his physiological state is racing at double, possibly triple, what was required of him prior to the ascent up the hill, but now he has slowed to a snail's pace. The brain of a child is much the same in highly charged interactions. The more frightening the outward experience, the higher the level of stress that will build in the brain, yet the child may seem to be moving at a slower pace, oftentimes even thinking slower. Reflecting is akin to the hill the biker is climbing. Until we thoroughly reflect, the hill continues to go on; steeper, higher, and more difficult. Relating is like the muscular output. It gets more and more difficult, the higher the hill becomes and the less experience we as parents have at reflecting. Regulating is the final eclipse of the hill when thorough reflection and relating has occurred. When they have both occurred in balance, then a natural downhill descent initiates. A child's primary needs in life are to be understood, and then loved. When the parent is able to reflect and relate, the child can feel understood. The parent gets in touch with his own fear and is then able to relate to the fear of the child. Once both have achieved a deep level of understanding, coasting down the hill becomes rewarding and cooling to the heated physiological system. Feel the hard-fought battle I am describing for you right now. Imagine the difficult climb, the sweat, and the pain. Now imagine the release of making it to the top and having a rewarding downhill breeze awaiting you.

Once the parent gets through his defensive fear reactions of taking the child's behavior personally, as a direct assault on his ego, then he is able to step into the role of regulatory teacher. When we, as parents, are in a state of dysregulation, we cannot teach regulation to our children. Look back on the incident with Jan and Susan. After Jan took the time to complete the Reflection Phase, she was able to begin the Relating Phase, and to convey a state of calm and understanding of Susan's feelings, instead of her usual habit of intervening while she was in a dysregulated state herself. As a result, Susan was able to reach a rapid state of regulation within herself, allowing her to go and bathe without the repetitive patterns that had been plaguing their relationship day after day.

After the Reflecting and Relating Phases, the Regulating Phase comes naturally. Therefore, there is no magical formula or a step-by-step approach within the Regulating Phase.

Pruning the Branches

A mother by the name of Sherri wrote me a very frantic e-mail one evening stating that her daughter was quickly slipping through her clutches. The daughter was becoming increasingly defiant and the mother was becoming increasingly frantic. The title of the e-mail was RELATE. The mother stated that she was not able to relate. She had done everything else, but her daughter seemed very angry and resistant.

I wrote back one very clear suggestion, "REFLECT!" That was it. I could feel the mother's anxiety level through the e-mail. It was high. What did that tell me? It told me that she needed to go back to phase one. She could not possibly have made it through Phase One successfully and have still been that frantic. In our society we want instant results. We have forgotten what it means to take time and think about a situation before acting on it. We have thoughts and we either act on them immediately, or out of fear, we do not act at all. Seldom do we reflect on why we want to move so fast or attempt to identify the fear that is stifling us.

Sherri wrote back a day later and stated, "That was all I needed. I realized how frantic I was and that I had jumped full gear into all of my own control issues again. I had even begun having recall of some trauma events in my life. I was stressed out and my daughter was taking it all in. Once I calmed down, then I was able to see how upset she was over the fact that her father and I are divorcing, and she feels responsible for him!"

The Three-Phase Intervention:
Reflect
- *Recognize the State*
- *Activate, the Internal System*
- *Feel, Feel, and Process*

Relate
- *Acknowledge the State*
- *Identify the State*
- *Support the State*

Regulate

Fertilizing the Field

"It has been remarked that in the final analysis every tragedy is a failure in communication." – Ashley Montagu

A farmer who adds fertilizer to his field is providing extra nutrients to ensure healthy growth of his crop. There are certain things we can offer our children that will provide the necessary "nutrients" for healthy family relationships.

Communication

Communication is a lost art. It is missing at home, at work, and in all of our other important relationships. As we discussed at the beginning of this book, we have forgotten how to communicate, primarily because of the technology age. Today, we spend so much time watching television and playing on the computer, that we no longer have time to talk to those around us, including our children.

Communication between parents and children is one of the most commonly neglected areas in our lives. As our children get older, one of the biggest differences that take place between family members is lack of communication. Gone are the days of "family time" when everybody sat down after dinner and talked about their day. These days we do not even talk during dinner because we no longer eat dinner together. Fast food and instant meals have taken over our lives. Not only is our health poorer than it has ever been in history, with the majority of children being considered obese when compared to children ten years ago, but our families are also in the worst shape in history.

As one mother stated, "When I was a kid growing up, not only did we eat together, we ate every meal together almost every single day of the week. My father was a farmer, so during the summer we had breakfast at 8:00 A.M., lunch at noon, and dinner at 5:30 P.M. Before bedtime we always had a small snack, and on occasion even this was eaten together. My mother always prepared healthy meals, not necessarily the exact amount of protein versus fat, but always a well-rounded meal at every sitting.

"As I got older, we maintained the same schedule. During the school year we had breakfast and dinner together, and we always got to talk. As I recall, those were some of the most pleasurable moments of my life. Also we never snacked between meals, and very seldom, if ever, did we eat out. I remember eating nearly everything on my plate each time, and seconds were always offered.

Fertilizing the Field

"Today, my husband leaves for work first and usually fixes his own breakfast. He always eats lunch on the go if he eats at all. I get the kids going, and while they are having cereal or some other high-sugar breakfast bargain, I'm getting ready for work. My breakfast consists primarily of coffee. I very seldom eat lunch. Our children normally have lunch at school, which is probably their best meal of the day.

"The evening meals depend primarily on where the family is and what our evening schedules look like. If you notice, I said "our schedules" because half of the time we all have very different plans for our evening. Definitely out is sitting down around the table to a nice pleasant meal. On most occasions I will cook and leave everything on the stove. Those who eat supper will fix their own plates and usually sit in front of the television or read a magazine. Those who don't like what's on the stove will just fix a sandwich. So goes our mealtime routine."

Unfortunately, this is a very common family scenario in which we not only look at a loss of quality family time, but we see poor structure and a diet leading to poor nutrition. However, the loss of family dinners is only one small way in which we have lost valuable communication time.

The importance of communication as discipline has to do with reinforcement, awareness, and prompting. Reinforcement in communication occurs when Mary and Sarah have been in Wal-Mart for Sarah's limit, and Mary says to Sarah, "Gosh, Sarah, you are doing a great job!" Mary has reinforced to Sarah that she is doing very well by riding nicely in the basket or walking right beside her. The underlying message that Sarah has processed is, "I'm a great kid because Mommy told me so, and because I'm a great kid I can ride in the basket!"

Next comes the awareness. After Mary tells Sarah how great she has been doing, she says, "We're going to be checking out in a few minutes; thank you for sitting so nicely." This is considered awareness in communication because Mary has made Sarah aware that they will be checking out soon, and she has made her mother very happy by participating in the shopping adventure. The underlying message that Sarah has processed is, "I'm important enough for my mommy to recognize my limits, and I can be a good helper when I feel good."

The last conveying factor in communication has to deal with prompting. When Mary says, "Thank you for sitting so nicely," she is essentially prompting Sarah to continue sitting nicely for the remainder of the shopping adventure. The underlying message processed by Sarah is, "I've done very well today, and I feel very good about myself."

You can grasp from this brief outline of a shopping adventure how the power of communication can go a long way in preventing the need for any disciplinary action. Also, this form of communication can be used in other areas such as road trips, outings, birthday parties, doctor visits, etc. It just takes communication to reinforce, to make aware, and to prompt. Communication is an essential aspect of parenting and discipline. Effective communication creates prevention.

Eye Contact

There are two very important components in our communication. These involve tone of voice and eye contact. We make so little eye contact when talking to our children that half of the time, if not more, they do not even realize we are talking to them.

To bring home this particular point while I am giving a lecture, I will begin by looking at someone in the audience and saying to them, "Right now you can tell that I'm talking to you because I'm making eye contact with you." Next, I will turn completely around and continue talking to that same person with my back to them and facing someone else. It is very difficult to feel or know that you are being talked to when there is no eye contact being made.

Children are the same. As long as we are not making eye contact, we cannot expect reciprocal behavior from them. At times, children will be unable to make eye contact because of the overwhelming sensory stimulation it invokes. In other words, they are doing the best they can to manage the stimulation in their bodies. Be mindful that when your child does not make eye contact, that rather than being disrespectful he may actually be really stressed and scared.

Reciprocal behavior is the ability to give and take in relationships. If I am talking to you, and you are not looking at me, then at some point I will get frustrated, stop talking, and say to you, "Do you really want to hear what I'm saying? If so, please look at me." When you are not looking at me, as far as I am concerned, you do not care about what I have to say. So I might as well save my words because to me they are very precious. I should not just waste them if you really do not care what I have to say.

Once while I was working with a mother and her adolescent daughter, I had gotten to the discussion of parenting and communication, when I realized they were not making any eye contact as they talked. I expressed the importance of communication and eye contact. After talking, we decided to do some experimenting. I told the daughter that she could leave the room. Then I said to the mother, "Okay, now go get your daughter and ask her to come sit down." The mom went to the door and yelled, "Joan, come here and sit down." Joan did not come. Again she said, "Joan, come back in the room." Of course, we were in their home, which allowed the environment to enhance the child's response. I intervened and told the mother to go to her daughter, touch her on the shoulder, make eye contact, and gently yet firmly say, "Come back and sit down with me." The child made immediate eye contact and sat down in the front room. I again dismissed the child, and we moved our experimental session to the kitchen table. This time I instructed the mother to talk casually to the daughter about school until I interrupted. Without wasting any of her words or emotional energy, the mother brought the daughter back in. While casually talking about school and the upcoming weekend, it was very clear that there was no eye contact between the mother and daughter. I instructed the mother to make proper eye contact, and within five seconds the daughter was again mumbling down to the table. Once again, I instructed the mother to dismiss the daughter, but this time to call her back when she got to the door. Amazingly, it was like the child never heard her. The child left the room, and the mother just sat staring at the door dumbfounded.

Suddenly, in a state of realization, the mother threw up her hands and excitedly exclaimed, "I get it, I get it! I need to make eye contact specifically, but I also need to use a tone of voice that will get her attention in order to be able to make eye contact!" I said, "Yes, you do get it!"

Again we tried the experiment. She went in the other room and called her daughter to the table where we were sitting. After a short discussion about expressing feelings when upset, I gave the mother the signal, and she dismissed her daughter. However, this time it was different. By the time Joan had made it to the door, Susan stated in a very strong voice, "Joan, one moment please." Immediately Joan stopped, turned around, and looked directly at Susan. In a very telling moment of their relationship, Susan said, "I love you, Joan," and Joan replied, "I love you too, Mom."

Tuning In

As in the example of Susan and Joan, there are several occurrences during an interaction that may lead to interference in communication.

To explain communication interference, I will use the analogy of listening to the car radio while driving. If the channel is not tuned in just right, you get a lot of static and no positive response; however, it may not be the radio's fault. There are several factors leading up to the interference. Some of the circumstances affecting the radio communication could be weather, location, or radio frequency. Until those factors are corrected, then it is difficult to get clear communication. Once all of the factors are cleared up, there will be beautiful music flowing from the radio.

How did Susan and Joan's communication resemble a poorly tuned station? Well, there are several ways. The first and biggest problem in the communication interaction of Susan and Joan was the same as it is for most parents.

Remember Parenting Points #1 and 2: Most historical parenting methods are ineffective. Also, Parents parent the way they were parented.

We have been taught to believe that if the radio is not tuning in correctly and giving us beautiful music, then obviously something is wrong with the radio. Furthermore, it is the radio's entire fault and has nothing to do with anything else. Like many parents, Susan was placing all of the blame for their lack of communication on Joan either not listening or being defiant. Parenting is not a blame game. It does not matter who is at fault. It only matters that the parents are the parents; therefore, it is their responsibility to find the solution.

In addition, Susan had been told that Joan was obviously suffering from *Oppositional Defiant Disorder (ODD)*, the popular diagnosis for an adolescent with a high fear response, or that she needed to be tested for *Attention Deficit Hyperactivity Disorder (ADHD)*. ADHD is the disorder parents are told their children have if they will not sit still for ten minutes and tune in to a teacher's lecture. This led Susan to believe that her daughter had some unconfirmed, mental-emotional disorder and she just needed to be fixed. Joan felt like she was not a good kid and was now crazy because she had a problem that she did not know how to correct.

Like the radio, we must tune in to our children. Start out by checking the weather (emotions). How are you feeling? Are you angry and frustrated? Sad? Depressed? The way parents feel communicates more to their children than what they say. If they are not feeling very positive, then they will not be using a strong voice to get their children's attention. If they are feeling angry, then they will be yelling or communicating spitefully, and their children will respond with fear or anger. Parents must check their own feelings first.

Second, check your location (are you in effective communication vicinity?). Is your child in another room? Are you making eye contact? Can your child see that you are talking to him? If you are not near your child when trying to effectively communicate with him, then he is not going to hear you, know that you are talking to him, or understand the importance of what you are trying to communicate. Therefore, you will continue to have communication interference.

Third, check the frequency (tone of voice). If, like Susan, your child has been conditioned to a certain decibel of sound, and you are not using the appropriate tone, then your child is not going to tune in appropriately. If you are communicating in a tone that is too soft, your child might not hear you. If you are using a tone that is too loud, then she will respond to the voice but not to the message. Check your frequency and make sure you are using the right tone of voice.

Last of all, after you have ensured that all of the other factors are not causing the problem, then.... CHECK THE RADIO! What could possibly be wrong with the radio? Maybe there's a loose wire (did not hear you!) or just a bad station (upset feelings!). If you are not tuned in to your child then you are bound to get bad interference. If you are trying to tune in to your child, and you have checked yourself over, then it is time to do some repair (listening!) and find out what is really bothering your child. Finally, after you get everything repaired and turn on the radio, the music should be really nice.

Now we are going to discuss the further ways in which communication can be utilized for effective and successful parenting.

Sharing Feelings

Feelings are similar to expectations. If you do not communicate to your child what you expect, then it is likely he is not going to meet your expectations. If your child does not know how you are feeling, then he cannot reciprocate to create a positive mutual exchange. The definition of reciprocate is to do, feel... in return. Without reciprocity then your feelings are neither acknowledged nor understood, which leads to upset feelings.

In order to communicate effectively, it is important to express both positive and negative feelings. If you only communicate to your child how good you feel, then eventually he will become insensitive to your negative emotions.

You would not believe how many times I have heard parents say they cry and express their hurt feelings. When I ask if they do this in front of their children, they get a real serious look on their face, sit up straight and say, "Of course not!" For some obscure reason we have been told not to let our children see us get upset because if we do, then they will feel like they have won. Since when did hurting someone's feelings become the indicator of victory?

If you do not show your children how you really feel, then how are they supposed to develop empathy and compassion for the feelings of others? A very popular parenting fad today is to "hold in" upset feelings at your child's inappropriate behavior and then proceed to respond in a fake manner without sounding too sarcastic. The goal is that the child will never see the parent get bristled. Instead he is given a consequence to make him take responsibility for his action. It makes perfect sense, right? Sure, if you want to raise a child with no empathy and complete disrespect for the feelings of others!

The cognitive psychology movement has been foremost in misguiding parents in their attempt to parent. Most of the parenting fads taught today are based on cognitive psychology such as teaching your child responsibility through logical consequences. The problem with the cognitive psychology movement is that it fails to include the rest of the body. *We are not merely thinking beings; we are thinking and feeling beings.*

In fact, some of the latest research has proven that our brains and bodies (thoughts, emotions, behavior) are in fact connected. Meaning if you are mad, then there are physiological changes occurring in your body that cause you to behave in a certain way. For the most part we have very little control over our physiological response. To test what I'm saying, go to the zoo and tell yourself over and over again that you are not going to flinch as you stand in front of the big ugly gorilla. Furthermore, tell yourself that when he hits the glass, not only are you not going to flinch, but you are not even going to move. You are using your cognitive processes to attempt to control your response. I guarantee you that as soon as the gorilla begins to move, you are going to back up. If not, when he hits the glass, you will certainly jump a foot off the ground. Even thinking about it makes the heart beat faster. These responses are due to the connection between our brain and body.

Not only is it okay to express your fear and other emotions to your child, but it is also vital to establishing a mutual, loving relationship. Remember how, as a child, when you fell and hurt yourself, you needed comfort. Imagine scraping your knee and then not telling anybody. You would most likely stuff your feelings down inside, and if stuffed repeatedly, you would begin telling yourself that no one really cares how you feel (due to having no reciprocity from others), and this could lead to lots of hurt, upset emotions.

Expressing Needs

What happens when you express how you feel to someone, and he tells you to just get over it or deal with it on your own? You usually feel worse. What happens when you express a need such as the need to be heard, and in return you are ignored? You will usually feel worse. You feel worse because having your needs met, acknowledged, and understood is equivalent to your self-acceptance. When communicating to your child, you at least want to be heard, and then you want or hope to be understood.

The same goes for your children. If they hurt themselves and they come to you for comfort, but your response is to push them away or say, "Oh, get tough and stop being a cry baby," they will stuff their hurt feelings deep inside. Stuffing feelings from unmet needs leads to problematic behavior, poor attitude, and difficult relationships. Not only are you saying to your children that it is not okay to feel hurt, but you are also communicating that they are not worthy of your affection and love. When I hear parents say, "If I let my child whimper and cry all of the time and cuddle him every time he gets hurt, then he'll never be tough," I get very frustrated. The toughness you create in your three-year-old will be the same toughness you are fighting when your child is eight, thirteen, or sixteen!

Once you begin communicating to your children what you need—eye contact, listening, doing their chores, etc., they will soon be able to express their needs to you. If we are unaccustomed to having our needs met, then it becomes difficult to express ourselves when we have a need. This occurs primarily due to a lack of trust that our need will be reciprocated. Communicating needs and expressing feelings take lots of time, work, and conscious effort; just like other aspects of parenting.

When working to express needs or feelings, sometimes it is important to focus on using phrases like "I need" or "I feel." We are unaccustomed to expressing needs and feelings, and others around us are equally unaccustomed to reciprocating needs. Therefore, when you look at your child and state, "I am really mad," do not allow him to take the focus off your feelings without acknowledging that he understands that you are mad. When your child says to you, "I am very mad," do not automatically respond defensively with, "Well, what did I do?" but rather, repeat his feeling by saying, "You are really mad." This validates how he feels, and then allows you to tune in to his anger and find out why he is upset.

Affection

Have you ever thought about how you feel when you and your child are holding one another on the couch, making really gentle eye contact, or just simply enjoying the sound of each other's voices? You probably feel warm and good inside, like eating a warm piece of Mom's chocolate cake right out of the oven. The problem is, we do not do this enough, and some parents do not do it at all.

Deep, meaningful communication is one of the most heart-felt ways to provide affection. Just stopping to say, "I love you" can fill our day with warmth and fulfillment. If we do not communicate our love to our children, then they fail to realize their self-worth and to develop a healthy self-image. Your child's self-image is the way he depicts himself as seen through your eyes, since you are his secure base.

In our society, demonstrating affection through communication is experienced even less than having a meaningful conversation. We may talk to our children all day long and not once say, "I love you," "You're doing a good job," or "Do you know that you're beautiful?" These are the affectionate statements that our children need to hear from us in order to provide them with wonderful colors with which they can paint their self-image.

Another aspect of affection that seems to fade away as children get older is physical affection.

Remember Parenting Point #2: Parents parent the way they were parented.

Affection is one area specifically influenced by our own parenting. The most common reason that parents do not demonstrate affection is because they were never showered with affection when they were children. Most families of generations past were working farm families. These families had a tendency to be very large, and everyone was required to help run the farm. In a number of situations, the older children would raise the younger children while both parents tried to make a living. Essentially, a child who was left in charge of the other children because both parents had to work did not receive an abundance of nurturance. When trying to care for siblings, the older child begins to take on the parent role. In such a case the older child who has not experienced nurturing himself is not capable of sufficiently nurturing the other children. Therefore, affection for these children becomes minimal. With such care, generation after generation, we have eventually produced parents who are uncomfortable with physical affection. I cannot think of a single person who does not enjoy and respond to a nice hug. I routinely treat adults who are starved for physical affection. If an adult is starving for affection, then quite naturally, he does not have enough to give to his children. A parent seeking to have his need for affection met by his child will eventually reject him in frustration. The parent will begin to feel that the child is unworthy because he is not meeting the parent's need for affection. As parents, we are responsible for giving affection to our children as a part of loving and nurturing them. We should reinforce that they give affection back. Returning affection is demonstrating reciprocity. However, we should not expect our children to meet the affection needs that our parents did not give us.

As the parent you, must make a conscious effort to demonstrate both verbally and physically to your child that he is loved and cherished. Say to your child, "I love you," and "You are very special to me." Give him lots of hugs, eye contact, and back rubs. These demonstrations of affection are very important to raising a healthy and responsible child.

Evaluative Behavior

Another important aspect of communication is evaluating behavior, which is essentially conveying to your child your own value system. Pointing out acceptable and unacceptable behavior is a part of good parenting. Communicating values creates within your child a sense of right and wrong. I call this sense of right and wrong the *Internal Morality Measuring Stick.* As children, our early experiences with our parents and with the outside world create within us as adults an ability to measure our behavior. According to our internal belief system, we either choose to act or not to act. This is the belief system we continuously fall back on throughout our entire lives. Not only will we utilize it ourselves, but we will also pass on the same value system to our children. *It is vital that parents understand that their actions will determine the way their children act toward their future children.*

For example, we have all heard about serial killers and mass murderers. Most recently we have listened to the stories of school kids killing other kids, blowing up schools, and beating up teachers. The early experiences of these people were not pleasant. Many grew up in the foster care system, witnessed violence, were traumatized, and sometimes abandoned. These adults, as children, failed to develop a sufficient sense of right and wrong. They experienced the world as a cold, mean place where they had to protect themselves from being hurt by others. Their Internal Morality Measuring Stick was not adequately developed. For most of these adults and children, their world was about self-preservation. Morally, they felt compelled to act in ways that determine self-preservation. Unfortunately, their acts were impulse driven without any type of moral support.

Evaluating behavior is an ongoing process in parenting, especially in our society. Children need parents to evaluate their behavior because, without it, they fail to create their internal measuring stick for morality. Often times you will find that when reading to your children, they will ask a lot of questions. Listen to what they are asking and how it applies to the response you give them. Sometimes they will ask, "Eeyore is being mean, isn't he?" Your response determines whether it is okay to say to a friend, "Well, my day was just fine until I saw you!" By evaluating behavior you say, "He's being very mean; that was an ugly thing to say!" Watch your children's reaction. Their eyes will focus on Eeyore. They will process what they have been told and see if it fits within the framework they have been taught.

We have allowed television to overrun our lives. It has consumed our communication by taking our time away from our children and replacing it with violence and fantasy. Furthermore, we as parents do not even watch television with our children. Everyone knows the influence that television, especially cartoons, has over a child. I can go and watch my three-year-old nephew after a series of action cartoons or Walker Texas Ranger, and he will be wired to the hilt: jumping around, kicking, punching, and full of energy.

When we do not watch television with our children, not only do we fail to sensor inappropriate sexual or violent content, but we also fail to provide a positive voice in evaluating behavior. A child who has no supervision while watching television is a child who feels like it is okay to hit, kick, and yell when angry. It is not hard to see. We are not paying enough attention. Evaluating behavior will allow you to censor and correct the negative elements on television that may later contribute to your child's morals and value system.

The same goes for computers and music. Both are huge parts of the pop culture, causing kids to flock to the Internet and music stores alike. If you do not already know the negative impact of the Internet on a young mind, then you should spend some time searching the web yourself. Although it is packed with lots of great information, without evaluative behavior, even your child can be attracted to the inappropriate sites.

In addition, music is no longer the poetic, happy melody and rhythm of the past. When I was a kid, rap music was just developing. Some music today is so violent and filled with hate that it is required to have an eighteen-years-or-older sticker placed on it. The problem is that stores cannot possibly censor what kids listen to. Most of the time, they do not even enforce the parental advisory sticker. So do not depend on others to do your job for you. Hopefully, most parents reading this book are not currently dealing with these social problems, but beware as your kids approach their teens. They will start to be led by peer influence if they do not have you to talk to them.

Here are a few guidelines for evaluating television, computers and music:

1. Do not allow your child to watch more than one hour of television per day. The one-hour of time should be part of a structured schedule.
2. Evaluate the channels on the television and permit your child to choose from two (preferably educational in nature, cartoons are too stimulating).
3. When at all possible, spend one hour watching with your child to increase time together and to evaluate any behaviors that are not appropriate.
4. Do not allow your child to play on the computer more than one hour per day. Permit only educational games or typing.
5. Unless your children are at least thirteen, they should not be on the Internet and then only with supervision.
6. Evaluate all music that your child listens to by listening to it first. When at all possible encourage classical, jazz, and soft music (if you start early, this will help greatly).
7. Take responsibility in being the teacher of your children and monitoring what they learn.

Your children need you to communicate to them about who they are, how they are doing, and what you think and feel they need to be doing. They need you to make eye contact with them because they really do care what you have to say. As the parent, you need to feel that what you have to say is important and then your children will feel it too. Evaluate their world for them. They will feel safer with you looking out for them.

Signs of Drought

In times of drought, the farmer's crop does not receive adequate nourishment. A farmer's crop can be destroyed if he is not prepared to recognize the early signs of drought approaching and make provisions for nourishment. There may be times when our children are not receiving adequate nurturing. We may get caught up in the busyness of day-to-life and lose our focus of tuning in to our children's needs and feelings. We may become preoccupied with an unexpected event in our lives and become emotionally unavailable to our children. Or we may slip back into some old habits of parenting the way we were parented. Any of these can cause a drought in our children's nurturing. Your children will usually let you know by their behavior when their needs are not being met, but I will include here a few forms of discipline that are telltale signs that you are entering into a dangerous drought.

Force

Many of the parenting techniques used today are what I refer to as *parenting by force*. All parents want their children to be respectful and obedient. But our children should respect and obey us out of love, not fear. Anytime we use our size to overpower our children, we are parenting by force, thus creating fear. Remember, you cannot overcome fear by creating more fear. The only way to overcome fear is through love. There are numerous ways parents use force to control their children. One such example is spanking.

Spanking is one form of discipline that I feel is ineffective and worthless. Also, if it is utilized consistently it is damaging and counter-effective. Once you spank, there is only one direction to proceed, and that is to spank harder.

Spanking is one method of discipline that most parents have either tried or have at least been tempted to try. Most every parent reading this manual has received at least one spanking. Why do I feel spanking should not be used?

On May 25, 1999, Oklahoma Senators passed a bill supporting parents who believed spanking was an effective method of discipline, even to the extent of leaving bruises. This last part fully supports what I just stated, "After you spank, you can only spank harder," hence you begin leaving bruises. Do I agree with spanking? Absolutely not! Do I feel that spanking is harmful? I most certainly do!

Historically, our society has condoned spanking as a tool for discipline, and has at times considered it the only tool recommended. As a society, we can look at our current state of existence and clearly see that changes need to be made at all levels and in all areas. I strongly believe that the practice of spanking as a form of discipline is one such area that needs changing.

There are very few adults and parents in society who are capable of using spanking for discipline without it being a direct projection of their own anger. We usually spank from a reaction of anger that is immediate and forthcoming, without thought or contemplation.

> *I recall the first and last time I ever gave my daughter a spanking. Early one morning as I was getting ready for school, and hurrying around trying to get out of the house before rush hour, my two-year old daughter walked in without her pull-ups on (I vividly remember being particularly stressed out that morning about a paper I had due). All of a sudden my daughter, standing right in front of me, started to pee on the floor. Now as I recall it, I do not even think she realized what she was doing because by this time she was quite enthusiastically using the potty. At first I was shocked, then out of anger I swatted her two times on the bottom and rushed her to the potty. As she sat on the potty with big crocodile tears rolling from her eyes, her big mean daddy realized how childish and immaturely he had just behaved. I tried to apologize, but the damage was already done.*
>
> *My response was totally out-of-line. I shamed and punished my daughter for a very natural part of the life of a two-year old. I lost my temper, not because my daughter had an accident, but because I was stressed out. My daughter does not even remember this incident, but it has stuck in my mind for years. Did my daughter ever have an accident again? Of course! Did I develop better ways to respond? You bet!*

The second reason I feel that spanking is not effective is because most children have not developed sufficient emotional self-control to communicate their feelings as opposed to acting them out. Self-control is a developmental process that is an aspect of maturity. It is not a learned or conditioned ability. Self-control is a desirable virtue; however, one cannot practice mind over matter if he does not have the brain maturity to begin with. If we genuinely want to be empathetic and understanding, then we will find out what is upsetting our child instead of spanking him for his actions.

Another very important reason that parents should not use spanking is because of the physiological "spiking" which occurs in the body's chemistry following such an emotionally overwhelming event. Can you remember ever feeling calm or feeling enlightened after a good whipping by your parents? I remember feeling very fearful; and then angry, resentful, hurt, and shamed. There were several occasions after I got a "whipping" (this is how my parents referred to my discipline), when I vowed to run away or never to talk to my parents again. I remember once after I was given a "whipping," that I got a hefty bag and commenced to pack all my clothes in it. About this time my father walked in. He saw what I was doing and said, "Oh, you're gonna run away, are you? How about if I give you another whipping?" I, of course, lied and made up some quick excuse about what I was doing. Needless to say, I did not get another whipping, nor did I run away.

I have used spanking as one example, but during any type of parenting by force, the body goes into a state of overdrive and self-preservation. The response is one of survival, not one of learning. The brain, while in a hyper-aroused state of functioning, cannot successfully incorporate an important message such as, "I am whipping you because I love you, and I want you to learn that it is not okay to break a window." Parenting by force increases the difficulty of learning. Research has found that the most ideal state for learning is calm arousal. Calm arousal is the state when you and your child are close to one another, calm, and relaxed. This is otherwise known as the state prior to sleeping. If you and your child are not in calm arousal, then he is not going to learn from your discipline. If you have to keep spanking your child time and again, then apparently he is not learning. Very few parents achieve positive results by using force. If a form of discipline is successful, the need for discipline will occur less and less frequently. This is not the case with parenting by force, such as spanking, where the child must be punished over and over again.

Deprivation

Deprivation is defined as taking away forcibly. There is no place for force in parenting. Remember, the only way to overcome fear is through understanding, awareness, and patience; which are all part of the essential practice of love. Anything that looks different than love comes from fear. It is very simple. You must not deprive a child of love, food, warmth, nurturing, learning, or life. I have heard horror stories of parents attempting to discipline by locking their children in the basement or in their rooms and only feeding them cold oatmeal because they would not eat their food. This is cruel and sadistic treatment for a child.

Remember the Ten Commandments and do not do anything to your children that you would not want done to you. Some children have traumatic responses that look like resistance or all-out defiance at mealtime when, in fact, they are responding to a physiological state of stress and fear, causing their emotions to prevent them from eating. In this situation, take a break from the table with your child, practice patience and breathing, and then process her emotions to find out what might be bothering her. Parenting is sacrifice, and your chicken just might have to go cold for a while.

Time-out

Time-out, without a doubt, is the most recommended and popular behavior-modification tool that has ever been prescribed to parents in their attempts to correct inappropriate behavior. Why is time-out a national phenomenon for parents? Time-out provides the parent, eager for change and consumed with an instant gratification mentality, with a simple, easy-to-use, quick fix to a momentary problem. By saying, "Uh, oh, you need a time out," a parent can take the child in the midst of a temper tantrum and place him in a chair in front of a wall for a specified period of time until he regains his composure and takes responsibility for himself.

Time-out essentially tells your child, "You are mad, hurt, or sad, and these are feelings that you need to deal with. I am going to isolate you with your feelings and let you do one of two things - either sort through them or repress them."

The child will process this message and conclude, "Okay, I have feelings, and I am being put in the corner away from everyone. Therefore, my feelings must be bad, which means I am bad." In response, the child will repress his emotions because he is not mature enough to process them rationally. Hence, *over a period of time he will come to fear his emotions. This will in turn lead to increased negative behavior.* Because all behavior stems from our internal stress, this will lead to the presence of the emotion of fear. If we keep hiding all of our fear, hurt and upset emotions; eventually they will resurface as destruction of property, whining, and temper tantrums in children; or as depression, hypertension, and cancer in adults.

In addition, repeated exposure to an environment where feelings are neither to be accepted nor expressed will routinely reinforce feelings of low self-worth. In other words, not feeling worthy will lead to low self-esteem and poor future relationships.

Threats

Can you recall from high school biology, Pavlov's theory of conditioning? In an experiment with his dogs, the scientist turned on a certain light just prior to the dogs being fed. Eventually, the scientist just turned on the light, and the dogs would salivate, even before receiving the food. This became known as classical conditioning. But what if Pavlov stopped feeding the dogs after turning on the light? Their response would eventually disappear. This is what typically occurs when parents threaten their children and do not consistently follow through. Eventually they are not going to respond to the threats!

The 1, 2, 3, method rarely works because sometimes we count beyond three and give our children additional chances to disobey. The children soon realize Mom and Dad are not going to enforce their threat. I will often say that instead of using 1,2,3 for the child, the parent should utilize it to calm himself.

Mom says, "Jake, turn off the television." Jake doesn't move. Again she says, "Jake, turn off the television." Jake doesn't move. This time she yells, "Jake, turn off the television!" Jake responds by saying, "Not right now, Mom, this is a good show." Various responses can occur at this point.

Mom acquiesces and either says, "Okay, but it's going off as soon as the show is over, or she says, "Okay, I'm counting to three, and the television better be off." The show ends or three arrives, and the television is still on, so she marches right over, completely flustered, and turns the television off. The same for, "Turn the television off or you're grounded!" The television is slammed off, and Jake stomps to his room. First, he was completely disrespectful by stomping to his room, and second, had you grounded him, it would probably have only lasted for a day.

Just like spanking, if something is working then you do not have to do it as often. If threats were followed by action, eventually the child would do as he was told the first time.

Inconsistency

One big area where parents fail in trying to teach or discipline their children is in not being consistent. Consistency is much the same as structure. Children have an inner need to feel secure and contained. Without having this inner need met, they feel insecure and out-of-control. By being inconsistent, we convey to our children that we are never quite certain of what we are going to do in a given situation. This leaves them unsure of how to act in this situation, which normally leads to an anxious or fidgety child.

It is quite common for a family to make a big decision like, "Okay, we're going to start having family time every evening at 6:00 P.M.!" The first evening it goes great, the second evening Dad has to work late, the third evening Mom is too tired, and by the fourth evening it is not even mentioned.

Your children's minds may work something like this without them ever saying a word: "Oh great, I'm actually going to sit down with both Mom and Dad and be listened to - this is great!" The second evening arrives, "Oh, well, at least Mom and I can be close and talk." The third evening, "I understand that Mom is tired. I can wait until tomorrow." By the fourth evening, "I think I'll just go to my room and lie down. I wonder if Mom and Dad really do want to spend time with me?" All of this can occur from being inconsistent.

The most common form of inconsistency, when it comes to limit setting, is failure to be consistent with discipline. For example, when your child does not turn off the television by the second request, you get up and turn it off. However, the next time the second request is made, you are too tired to get up and turn it off, so you forget about it, and your child continues watching television. Later that week, you again request that your child turn the television off, and after the first request is completely ignored, out of anger you turn the television off, pick your child up by the arm, and give five firm swats. You yell and cry that he never listens to you, and then send him off to his room.

Inconsistency is a reinforcing and self-fulfilling prophecy. By continuously ignoring, overlooking, and rationalizing behaviors that you have already deemed unacceptable, you are ensuring that they will continue to arise time and time again.

Bribery

Bribing my child! What are you talking about? I never bribe my child! Have you ever gone to Wal-Mart and said with an anxious tone, "If you will be nice in the store, I'll buy you a toy." Of course you have, and that is bribery. Essentially you are bribing your child into better behavior.

What happens to the criminal who bribes the crooked cop? Over time the price of looking the other way gets higher and higher. Before long the cop is looking for a way to get more bribes, and the criminal is looking for a way to get rid of the cop.

I once listened to a mother tell me how good her son was doing since she started the new behavior-modification chart. Yes, the son's behavior had improved temporarily, but the mother was also spending an extra thirty-five dollars a week on Pok-e-mon. As the mother told me of the improved behavior, she also worriedly added, "But this sure is getting expensive!"

The purpose of behavior modification is to modify the inappropriate behaviors in small increments until the child has become conditioned to behave in a more appropriate manner. The problem with including positive reinforcement in a behavior modification plan is that it conditions the child to think the reward is more important than the behavior. So later when there is no immediate reward being offered, out of anger and a sense of betrayal, the child will revert to his old ways.

Behavior modification with positive material rewards is the same as bribery. Your child should learn to behave out of love and respect, not out of bribery and material gain.

Consequences

One common approach to parenting is attempting to provide your child with logical consequences in a caring way. For instance, the child shows defiance and says he is not going to do his homework. In a loving way the parent says to the child, "That's just fine, but you'll have to live with the bad grade. And you know what bad grades mean - no allowance!" The parent then goes away and leaves the child sitting helplessly and wondering what the best decision should be; hence, using logical consequences. A closer look at this situation will show that there were two types of consequences applied. A bad grade is the logical result of neglecting homework, while no allowance is a parent-formulated consequence.

There are actually three types of consequences to consider. *Natural Consequences* occur as a natural result of a choice or behavior. These pertain mostly to the laws of nature. For example, if a child rides his bike down a hill too fast, he may fall and get hurt. This type of consequence is unplanned and inevitable. These consequences occur naturally in everyday life and are very successful at changing behavior without any parental intervention. *Logical Consequences* occur as a logical result of a choice or behavior and are directly related to it. For example, if a child rides his bike down a hill too fast, his mom may put his bike away until he is mature enough to be more cautious. This type of consequence may occur automatically or the parent may apply it. These consequences are not as successful as natural consequences, but they can be useful at times. *Parent-formulated Consequences* occur by the decision of the parent. For example, a mom may tell her child that each time he rides his bike down the hill too fast he is going to have to do 50 push-ups. This type of consequence is assigned arbitrarily by the parent and does not relate innately to the child's choice or behavior. These consequences are not only hard to enforce, but they are unsuccessful in achieving the desired result. *I do not recommend using parent-formulated consequences.*

There are some popular parenting approaches that have falsely claimed that they use natural or logical consequences, when in reality, they are encouraging parents to formulate their own consequences. The only types of consequences that are useful as a learning tool occur automatically, so there is really no use for parents to spend their time trying to dream up creative consequences for their child's behavior. It is more important for parents to put their effort into empathizing with their child and understanding their child's behavior in terms of their stress level.

All behavior stems from stress, which creates fear. Whenever a parent walks away from an upset child, the parent is leaving him to deal with his fear alone. His goal is that the child does not see him get rattled, and then that the child decides for himself what should be the best course of action. In reality, it demonstrates to the child that his mom or dad does not care about his feelings because if they did, they would have asked him why he is upset and would have listened to his answer.

If a child is upset enough that he is not doing as the parent asks him or he is not meeting his responsibilities in the home, then the parent has to take responsibility by finding out what the child is upset about. The basic shortcoming of the very popular approach that claims to use logical consequences (which are actually parent-formulated consequences) is that it fails to address the genuine cause of the problem or misbehavior. It is important to feel understood. A lack of understanding leads to ignoring feelings, which leads to unmet needs. Needs that go unmet eventually lead to fear-based behavior. *Also, a key point to remember is that when your child is defiant, disrespectful, and disobedient, he is not feeling very connected to you. Disconnecting produces anger, loneliness, fear, and sadness.*

A Bountiful Harvest

We shall end where we began by concluding, "Parenting is Difficult." Each day with our children is a day that requires more of us than the day before. What can we do with this understanding? Realize that we as parents are the critical element to raising our children. We are the farmers of our gardens, the tenders of our crops. Notice that I have never mentioned planting the seeds, because our children have been planted in the gardens God has chosen for them. It is our responsibility to take the seeds that have been planted in our lives, nurture them, be patient with them, and harvest them when it is time, giving birth to a crop of abundance and wealth. This, my fellow parent, is the work of the world. If we are to make our world a place of beauty rather than pain, and love opposed to fear, it starts with us as parents.

Take the time necessary to renew yourself for the upcoming day. Look in the mirror and tell yourself:

"I am a good parent. I am a strong bow setting forth viable and capable arrows. I am the farmer of my garden and upon these banks I shall grow a tender and ripe fruit. I shall allow these sacred waters to nurture this crop, provide for it those sacred elements, and from that place I will guide it into life."

In one of his "Seven Habits of Highly Effective People" trainings, Dr. Stephen R. Covey tells a story:

It was a dark and stormy night. The officer on the bridge came to the Captain and said, "Captain, Captain there is a light in our sea lane, and they won't move." The Captain responded, "What do you mean they won't move? Tell them to move. Tell them starboard right now!" The signal was sent out, "Starboard, starboard." The signal came back, "Starboard yourself!"

"I can't believe this. What's going on here? Let them know who I am," the Captain responded in disbelief. The signal was sent out, "This is the Mighty Missouri, starboard." The signal came back, "This is the lighthouse!"

Dr. Covey goes on to state, "Correct principles are lighthouses; they do not move. They are natural laws. We cannot break them; we can only break ourselves against them. We might as well learn them, accommodate them, utilize them, and be grateful for them, then it enlarges us and emancipates us and empowers us." *For All Things A Season* is based on correct principles. You will find that in the midst of change as a parent, you will want to be the one to give up, even though your child will seem to be responding in a positive manner. Be strong and accept the child training duties that God has given you and persevere through the tough times. The tough times are what make us stronger!

Questions and Answers

O ver the years I have spoken with hundreds of parents about various parenting issues. In this closing section I have provided answers to some of the most common questions asked. Some of the answers might need to be modified to fit your particular question. There is no solution that can be applied to every situation, but there are some general principles that we can apply to most of them. All children and families are different in personality and style; however, the one thing we all have in common is that we all want someone to love and care for us. These answers are not definitive solutions to all problems—merely guidelines to follow in similar situations.

Q: At what age should I begin using The Three R's?

A: Practice of The Three R's is beneficial for children and adults no matter what the age. Remember Point #9 - *The only true change, is change within oneself.* A part of the power of The Three R's is the focus on internal awareness and change rather than trying to change others.

Q: Where should I practice The Three R's?

A: Being mindful of one's internal processing should be a constant action rather than a reaction to a negative situation. The Three R's can be practiced anytime in any place. I often tell parents during the really difficult times, that the most important and beneficial thing they can do is to stop and breath. It is our fear that prevents us from doing such.

Q: What should I do when my child starts acting out in a store?

A: Your strategy should begin before you even reach the store. Remember to pre-plan, set expectations, and communicate. Keep your child in arm's reach at all times. If dysregulation occurs, you want to be right there to correct it. Stores are also a good place for utilizing Time-In. Most parents are not proactive enough when it comes to correcting store misbehavior. If you realize there is going to be a problem, then park your basket in a side aisle and go to the car for some Time-In. Once your child has become regulated, then it should be safe to complete your shopping. However, if you allow your child to run wild in the store, then do not expect him to stay calm and regulated.

Questions and Answers

Q: My six-year-old will not go to time-out, what should I do when this occurs?

A: The first thing you need to do is read Chapter 6. Second, don't use time-out. Use time-in.

Q: My eight-year-old son loves to snuggle with me. Is this normal?

A: It is great if your child does not resist you and in fact likes being close to you. The important thing to watch for is how he responds to you when he is scared and upset. This is when most of the resistance might arise. A child with a tendency toward hypo-arousal, will enjoy closeness during the times when he is calm, but when he becomes upset and frightened, he will feign distance, becoming more passive, withdrawn and quiet. If this occurs, show him that you can accept his upset feelings as well as his good feelings. By doing this, he will feel even closer to you.

Q: Until recently, my child has not had any problems sleeping alone. Now he has started coming into our bedroom in the middle of the night. What should we do?

A: I suggest walking with him back into his room and soothing him back to sleep. Children wake up for various reasons during the night, and most times they just need a little added comfort. If your son has not normally had a problem sleeping, then talk to him and find out what might be bothering him when he wakes up.

Q: As a single dad raising a daughter, I sometimes feel that I should not show her too much affection because I do not want to give the appearance of doing anything inappropriate with her. How should I handle this?

A: As a single dad you have two roles - mother and father. Do not be afraid to show your daughter as much affection as you possibly can. There is a big difference between loving touch and mean touch. You can never give a child too much loving touch. Also as a single father, the more affection you show your daughter now, the less likely she will be to seek affection from others before she is ready. She also needs attention from adult women who can act as role models. Talk to your mother or female relatives or friends who have children. They should be delighted to help you out.

Q: My four-year-old enjoys performing at home so we decided to put her in dance classes. She did fine until the recital. She started crying and became very clingy towards me. When we got home she would not tell me what was wrong. What should I have done?

A: It sounds like your daughter, although quite comfortable at home, is not yet ready for the big lights. Often times during the midst of a stressful expression children actually will not know what is wrong or what they are feeling. Sit patiently with your child, and listen to her expression without judgment. Remember that underneath any behavior is stress, which gives expression to the emotion of fear. Sometimes it is beneficial just to be aware of the presence of fear and soothe your child without talking to her. Next time, try talking to your child before the recital about how she is feeling. This will help her to regulate any anxiety that might be building up. Sometimes pageants, recitals, and plays are just too much too soon. Do not push her if she is not ready.

Q: All of my friends tell me my children fight because they are so close in age, and I should just let them fight it out. What do you think?

A: Sibling rivalry should never be viewed as normal. Sibling rivalry occurs due to the continuous presence of fear, with minimal interruption. In other words, children will start to fight once they have been out of the parent's presence for some time. Often times I encourage parents to limit the time their children play with one another for a while, and then start to rebuild it slowly within their tolerance. Also, I recommend that parents be nearby when the siblings are playing. Just their presence alone will create an atmosphere of safety and a feeling of security for the children.

Q: I seem to be arguing with my six-year-old over everything. What can I do?

A: First of all, as the parent, you need to realize that you do not have to argue with a child. As the parent, you must feel deeply within yourself that you can make the right decisions for your child based on love and compassion. Often times when parents find themselves arguing with their children, they will notice that they are feeling scared themselves. Sometimes it is just the fear of making a mistake! Calm yourself and let your child know that you can make the right decision and she does not have to agree with you. Empathize by letting her know that sometimes giving up control is scary. Be patient and move slowly with your child, without trying to force or coerce her into agreeing with your opinion because of your fear. Love does not need coercion - it simply exists. Listen to your child's opinions as well; she may actually have a good point.

Q: My son seems angry most of the time. I know that teens are supposed to be difficult, but this is ridiculous. I have tried parenting techniques recommended in books, but those only seem to make him more resentful. What do you suggest?

A: I believe two of the most common periods of difficulty for children are the two's and the teen's. Brain research demonstrates that it is during these two critical periods that the brain is most active. For toddlers, the brain is rapidly expanding. For teens it is pruning away everything it has not used–. In essence, it is getting smaller. Remember the two primary emotions - *love and fear*. Look past your child's anger, no matter how big he is, and see his fear. Imagine all of the rapidly changing elements of his world, the demands, the homework, the push to consider college, and how all of these dynamics work together to create an enormous amount of stress. For the next two weeks, seek only to understand your son. Spend an extra thirty minutes every single day just trying to understand him. This does not mean lecturing, but listening. Do this for two weeks and then evaluate the situation. I am sure you will see such a dramatic change that you will want to continue in this manner.

Q: My ten year old has begun urinating in very inappropriate places such as in the corner of the living room. What is this all about and what on earth can I do about it?

A: Elimination is yet another highly misunderstood behavior when it comes to children. Oftentimes, this behavior is portrayed as the child being very angry with the parent and then in a metaphorical manner, peeing on the wall or floor as symbolism for peeing on the parent. This, I'm afraid, is a very abstract concept, in that during times of high stress, our thinking becomes confused and distorted. What this behavior indicates to me, rather, is a very stressed out and scared child. I suggest that the next time this extreme behavior occurs, you recognize immediately that your child is feeling overwhelmed and terrified. Go to her without even mentioning the incident and give her a hug. Tell her how much you love her and then ask her to come and spend time with you. Talk to her about what she may be feeling until both of you feel better. Tell your child that if ever she is ever feeling scared or needing a hug she can come to you and just let you know. Afterwards, go in the room and clean up the mess without ever mentioning it to her. Try this once and see the difference.

Q: My son lies about everything. What can I do about this?

A: I have developed a very simple formula for helping families to overcome lying. If you are willing to commit yourself to this formula for two weeks, I can guarantee you will see a dramatic difference. First of all, remember the two basic emotions - love and fear. A lie is an indicator of fear and stress. This is the formula: *Ignore the lie; do not ignore the child.* As soon as your child tells you a lie, do not even acknowledge it. Walk to him slowly, give him a hug, tell him you love him and you always will, and then walk away. If you have time ask him to spend some time with you. Just ask him how he is feeling, how he is doing, what he is thinking, etc., but do not acknowledge the lie. Later, when your child is calm, say to him, "It really hurts my feelings when you tell me a lie." This statement is very powerful for teaching empathy and trust through love rather than fear.

Q: My child has been given a diagnosis of Reactive Attachment Disorder because of her behavior. I adopted her at two, and she is now twelve. Most of the therapeutic and parenting advice for this disorder advocate that the parent "must be in control" of the child. What are your thoughts on this?

A: To begin with, labels are dangerous. Do not allow anyone to put a label on your child because this only creates fear and puts her heart in a box based on behavior she is demonstrating when she is the most afraid. Now for your question, "control" is fear-based. The only time we seek to control is when we, as adults, feel threatened or afraid. When professionals recommend that parents "be in control" they are playing a fear-based blame game without ever knowing it. First, you are told you must be in control, meaning you cannot let your child control you (fear #1). Then, if you are not in control, you must be to blame (fear #2). If that happens, you must not be a good parent (fear #3), or worse still you have a damaged child (fear #4). Fear breeds fear. Unfortunately, this is the basis for most mental health treatment, so please do not take this out against your practitioner. Practice the Three R's. Once you are able to reflect you will find yourself feeling less threatened; hence, you will feel less inclination to control your child, but rather you will be in a light of understanding. From the perspective of understanding, you will find yourself to be empowered to connect with your child. It has been said that the man who controls himself, controls the key to the universe. Reflect on your feelings and come to feel the power you hold within. Once you feel less threatened, your child will feel less threatened and her behavior will change quite naturally.

Q: We have an adopted child. We adopted him at one and he is now eight. Am I imagining things, or is he angrier with me than with my husband. It seems he directs all of his anger at me, but adores the ground my husband walks on. Help me to understand this behavior.

A: Unfortunately, this is another widely misunderstood behavior of adopted children. It is believed that because they were given up by their biological mother, they are angry and now direct all of their anger towards their adopted mother. I suspect that rather than the child directing his anger towards the mother, he is in fact overly sensitive to fear and stress because of his early trauma. When you combine this with the fact that more than likely he spends more time with the mother than the father, and the mother may have some of her own unresolved issues about adopting, you have a formula for a very strenuous and fear-based reaction. The rhythmic patterns between the mother and child become frayed with fear. The child begins to believe that the mother does not love him and the mother begins to believe that she is not a good mother. These distorted thoughts create escalating and continuous states of fear. At this point, I ask the mother to get in touch with her deeper fear and from that perspective, connect with an understanding of her child's fear. The mother can communicate this fear and they can process it together, which brings soothing, understanding, and a renewed commitment for connection.

Q: Sometimes my child will go hours refusing to eat. After a while I begin to worry, but when I offer food she usually will say, "No, not hungry," or will want to continue playing. Food has become a major issue for us. What do you suggest? Is she old enough to have an eating disorder?

A: I have spent increasing amounts of time with many parents regarding this very issue and often times the problem is the fear of an eating disorder being present or a complete misdiagnosis by a clinician. I was recently on a home-visit with a family during dinner time. The family consisted of a mother and her five-year old daughter. The child had been eating just fine until she suddenly became fidgety, active, occupied with everything other than food. Upon asking her what was wrong, she responded by saying she had a "brain chill!" Imagine this from a five year old. I must remind you however that this is the most gifted child I have ever had the honor of working with. So, I asked her to tell me what that meant and she responded, "Sometimes when my brain gives me a chill, I can't eat. My body wants to eat but my body won't let me." I believe that we can use the advanced verbal abilities of my little client to look deeper into what often occurs for children. Her statement only validated what I had seen before in my work. When children get overloaded in their sensory systems it creates a food-related disconnection between body and brain. Meaning, the body says yes, but the brain says no! Stress causes the disconnection.

My suggestion is first to reflect on your own internal state as the parent and be aware of your fear related to this issue. Once you are centered, listen to the behavior. There will be times when you will need to sit your child beside you without trying to engage her to sit still or even to eat. Allow her to color a picture or any activity that might foster her ability to be present at the table. During this time, take her food and slowly feed it to her without bringing unnecessary attention to your feeding actions. If the brain is engaged in other activities and the body is truly hungry then her little mouth will open and accept the food. In addition to this, always attempt to practice prevention by being mindful of your child's state of behaving before mealtime. Create an environment of calm around this otherwise hectic time. Doing so will bring calmness into your child's state of being before food becomes the focal issue. Last but never least, work diligently to be mindful of your own internal state of being.

Q: I have been told by family members and by teachers that my son needs to be on medication for his mood swings and hyperactivity. Some have said that he seems to be bi-polar and others have mentioned ADHD. What would you suggest?

A: Before putting any child on medication I advise you to read "Reclaiming Our Children" and "Toxic Psychiatry," by Peter Breggin, M.D. Dr. Breggin is a psychiatrist and leading authority on the fight to keep kids off dangerous and toxic psychiatric medications. In my opinion, your child would receive more benefit from a change in the structure of his environment and routine rather than anything else. In addition, psychiatric labels can be as dangerous as the medications themselves when it comes to our views in society. Such labels are very blame-oriented and disempowering to children and families. Often times they hinder our natural abilities to make changes within ourselves and our direct environment, but rather place a focus upon children as being unreachable or worse yet, having malfunctioning brains.

I encourage you to watch your son closely over the course of a week and identify the specific times of day that his mood swings seem to occur. Furthermore, observation of his school routine should help you to determine the class and time in which he seems to become increasingly hyperactive. Analyze these times and try to determine what modifications can be made within the environments that might help him better adjust and relax, prior to the time in which the emotional shifts occur. Also, start spending twenty minutes of uninterrupted time with your son each day. Do this for two weeks and then make another observation of any shifts in his behavior. If you have not witnessed a dramatic change after this time, e-mail me and I would be more than willing to help you explore other options.

Grafting Branches

Grafting a branch involves moving it from one parent branch to another, joining them together to become one plant or tree. Farmers often use this method in order to improve their crops or produce a new variety. The grafted branch draws its nutrients from the root of the parent plant or tree. Many of the children I see in my work have been grafted into their families through foster care or adoption. Many of them have a history of neglect or abuse before being adopted. Without the farmer's intervention, trees of a particular variety will always produce fruit of that same variety. In much the same way, children raised in a traumatic environment, will grow up to create trauma for their own children, because they have drawn their nutrients from the roots of an unhealthy parent plant. This will continue generation after generation unless this cycle is stopped by either the parent becoming healthy or by the child being adopted or placed in quality foster care. Even if these children are grafted into a foster or adoptive family, we must make sure that the new family has healthy roots that provide the proper nutrients for a healthy child. All of these recommendations I have described so far apply to foster and adoptive families as well, but I have included some additional information in this chapter that applies specifically to children with a history of early trauma.

The following are articles I have written previously for other publications and web sites. They have been included here in an effort to assist parents of children who have been adopted, are in foster care, or have experienced trauma and are struggling at home and in the school environment.

When Beauty becomes the Beast

Children's behaviors can be, at best, difficult to understand. Negative behaviors can be even more difficult to understand, especially when we have little insight into the causative factors. Adopted children will often exhibit behaviors such as lying, stealing and defiance; and parents may have little awareness as to why they are behaving this way. Faced with such challenging behaviors, parents often feel helpless. The beautiful child brought into the home for love and security, can quickly turn into the Beast.

In writing this article I hope to provide the reader with a view of the inner workings of the adopted child's brain/body system, its response to being separated from biological parents, and its learned reactions to early trauma exposure. If you are an adoptive parent, my hope is that after reading this article, you will be better equipped to look at your child in a different light, a light of increased awareness and understanding. You will have a better understanding of the causative factors behind your child's behavior, allowing you to be more available to help your child heal from the early exposure to separation and trauma.

In this article, I will make many references to the brain/body system rather than to solely the brain or the body. My belief is that the brain and body are inseparable, and work in harmony with one another. For instance, when you feel panic, your brain sends a signal through your body, your pulse accelerates and your body temperature fluctuates. It is with this fundamental knowledge of brain and body behavior that I have been able to pioneer an approach to family treatment that has proven to be highly successful and mutually rewarding to both parent and child. I hope my interpretations will assist you in your task of parenting your child more effectively.

Stress is a common occurrence in daily life. It is an unavoidable natural aspect of our existence. In a healthy situation stress activates the brain/body system to protect, assist, work, live and love. Stress can be the driving force behind our basic need to achieve a healthy state of well-being. When stress becomes prolonged, overwhelming, or chronically unpredictable, it transforms itself into trauma. If stress becomes pervasive, uninterrupted, or out of control, damage can occur to the brain/body system. Consequently, the brain may become unable to shield itself against this bombardment of stress. Once the brain senses that an environmental threat such as abuse is unpredictable or overwhelming, the brain will make the necessary adaptations to defend itself. Those adaptations usually manifest themselves in the form of extreme sensitivity, aggression and disconnecting.

When an adopted child has experienced trauma in her early formative years, she is left with a very scared monster lurking inside her brain/body system that I call the "Beast." Though ghastly and threatening in appearance, this Beast is simply a terrified creature that is constantly on guard, trying to defend the "Beauty" hidden beneath the Beast. The Beast is with her always, waiting for the time when the child feels threatened or afraid. It is at this moment that the Beast roars to life. Seemingly out of nowhere, the Beast erupts from within and Beauty is nowhere to be found.

Adopted children who have experienced early, recurrent trauma are, by their very nature, sensitive children. They are often more sensitive than biological children, but until recently, not much thought has gone into why this occurs. For these children, the initial break from their biological parents is an area that has received scant attention from the scientific community in the past. Recent research has shown that this initial break is, in fact, traumatic to the infant's brain/body system. Regardless of the environment in which the child is placed, the physiological break from the biological parent is an overwhelmingly stressful event. Such an event could be compared to the terror a small child may feel when he finds himself suddenly lost in the middle of the shopping mall. An immediate sense of panic pervades, the parent is lost amongst all of the other shoppers and the child feels scared, alone, and helpless! Even the comfort of a stranger is only reassuring to the extent that the child may momentarily stop crying. However, in this type of situation, the parents are eventually found, and the child is restored into the calm containment of his parents' arms. For the adopted infant who has been removed from his biological parents, his cry is the signal of his immense pain and fear. Therefore, when the cry of that infant quiets we naturally assume that he is comforted. Unfortunately, that is rarely the case for this child. As we examine the impact of early stress on the brain /body system, consider the implications of such an experience.

The extraordinary sensitivity demonstrated by an adopted child stems from her early exposure to stress, which has usually resulted in trauma. As the brain/body system continues to be bombarded by traumatic events such as loss of a biological parent, neglect, abuse, lack of physical contact or prenatal drug exposure, it adapts itself to this stressful environment. The brain/body system will work diligently to protect itself from any future harm. We must remember that the threat/stress sensor inside the brain is fear-based. This means the immediate primary emotion of the human species is, in general, that of fear. As the exposure to threat and stress continues, the brain/body system responds in a manner similar to persistent terror. Over a period of time, the stress-producing events may diminish or even cease, but by this time it is probably too late. The brain/body system has adapted and is prepared to react. If the exposure to trauma has occurred during the period between conception and thirty-six months, the brain pathways form around the negative adaptation, locking into place a highly sensitive brain state, in order to be on guard against future threat. Hence, the Beauty becomes the Beast anytime she feels threatened or scared. The fear response can begin in a millisecond and can be triggered through any of the sensory pathways (sight, sound, touch, taste, smell, or temperature).

With this new understanding of the brain/body system and its effects on your child's behavior, you should be able to see your child from a new perspective that is rarely offered. A screaming, kicking, biting child should no longer be viewed as an angry, out-of-control child; but rather, a child who is scared by some trigger within his immediate environment and is solely dependent on the stress reactions his brain/body system has learned from exposure to early trauma. Research demonstrates that in times of high stress, our cognitive thinking becomes greatly distorted, leaving us susceptible to high states of emotional arousal with little clear thought. Therefore, in addition to having a child who is highly dependent on his learned stress-response, you also have a child who is incapable of demonstrating the ability to have clear and effective cognitive thinking in the midst of perceived threat.

In closing, I would like to add that when parenting an adopted child it is imperative to consider traumatic experience or exposure and its subsequent effect on your child. A view focused solely on child behavior will lead to feelings of parental rejection, blame and helplessness; undoubtedly causing the same feelings within the child. I encourage you to work diligently to view your child from the perspective that her brain/body system is creating a constant sense of threat or even terror within her. From this perspective, I am certain that you will come to a deeper understanding of your child's behavior and you will be equipped to take the steps necessary in making her feel less threatened. In doing so you will assuredly create an environment of increased security and acceptance, resulting in a calmer state of the brain/body system, which will in turn diminish negative behavior.

Education and the Child of Trauma

S chools are filled with children who are victims of recent trauma or have a life filled with trauma. The violence witnessed by youth in some communities has become so pervasive that in some studies over half of all children surveyed had witnessed some form of violence in the year prior to the survey.[1] Educators face this student body without the understanding necessary to enable children to access the appropriate cognitive experiences. Cognitive education has always been the school's primary responsibility. Social and emotional learning, we hope, are primarily the parent's domains. Ideally, it is the family that teaches children values, morals, and respect for others. However, oftentimes it is the family that is the primary source of trauma. It has been estimated that more than 250,000 students are attacked in school each month.[2] This article was written to assist school systems in gaining a better knowledge of the child with a trauma history, within the educational environment. This article is written from the premise that the primary task of the educational system is to provide children with appropriately-based cognitive experiences. It must be understood that cognitive education is generally the primary responsibility of schools, with social and emotional learning as an essential by-product to the direct learning environment provided.

Early Exposure to Trauma

The early exposure to traumatic experience, especially during the time frame from conception to age three, exposes the developing neurophysiological system to what can be termed as "arrested emotional development." The environment of calm interaction between parent and child is necessary to the successful development of the brain/body tools for emotional *regulation (the state of calm functioning)*. When this is absent, the normal and healthy developmental experiences are missed. This absence of calm interaction creates a response of chronic stress and the child is essentially left without soothing. In this manner, the developing child continuously experiences stress during the time when he should be experiencing calm interaction. The resulting outcome is an individual system that is poorly equipped

---

1 Statistics cited from Child Trauma Academy 2001. Surviving Childhood: An Introduction to the Impact of Trauma. Child Trauma Academy.com

2 Statistics cited from Child Trauma Academy 2001. Surviving Childhood: An Introduction to the Impact of Trauma. Child Trauma Academy.com

for tolerating and managing stressful environments. Due to the presence of a stimulating environment and the absence of the parent figure, school can be a highly stressful experience for such children. The difficulty is not in the feeling of stress that is triggered by the stressful environment, but rather the emotional state of fear that these children feel. The brain and body respond to stress inwardly, but this translates cognitively into fear, which triggers the fight, flight or freeze response.

The specific receptor in the limbic system equipped for responding to threats is the amygdala. The amygdala responds automatically to any manner of threat. For example, in a situation where a child becomes scared, a fear reaction occurs immediately. This is an automatic reaction of the amygdala. Conversely, the hippocampus is the area of the limbic system responsible for determining how stressful the situation truly is. In this manner, the hippocampus acts as the fear regulator, the component ultimately responsible for effective stress regulation. The hippocampus then communicates to the rational area of the brain and makes the decision whether to calm down, fight, freeze, or flee. The hippocampus allows the child to think in the midst of the experience, "Well, maybe this is not so scary after all." Therefore the child calms down and is no longer frightened.

Brain research leads us to believe that the amygdala forms while still in the womb. The hippocampus, on the other hand, is developing throughout the critical early period of infancy. In this manner, if the environment has been overly stressful and lacks effective parental regulation at an early age, the hippocampus becomes stagnated in its growth. Hence, the term "arrested emotional development." Ultimately, this leads to an amygdala that pours out stress and a hippocampus that is so poorly developed that it is unable to determine to any successful degree, how stressful the event may truly be. As a result, the stress and relating fear escalate, and the rational processes become confused and distorted. Bruce Perry has referred to such a state in children as an "amygdala hijacking." The amygdala pumps out stress and fear in an uncontrollable manner, and the child is essentially held hostage to his own neurophysiology.

As this child continues to grow, his emotional system remains under arrest. This continues until an environment conducive to constant regulation has been provided. Once such an environment has been provided, the slow, tedious process of reparative stress interaction begins to occur. The developing system begins to learn some degree of emotional regulation throughout each day, but overly stressful interactions send this highly sensitive system rapidly back into old patterns of chronic, intensified fear that is triggered by the stress reaction. For example, an inmate is let out of jail on probation under constant supervision and positive interaction; however, with any lack in supervision the highly sensitive inmate is quickly drawn into the wrong crowd, and before long ends up back in jail. This prospect of providing an environment conducive to constant regulation becomes increasingly difficult for parents, and over time the supervision becomes lax and the interaction not nearly as positive; therefore, the developing system is rarely allotted the necessary environment to overcome the powerful effects of the early trauma (stress) exposure.

School Time Challenges

Eventually, the child becomes of school age. The operative word here is school "age". Due to the effects of the early traumatic (stressful) environment, the child's emotional ability is nowhere near the appropriately functioning ability of a school-ready child. Placing this child in school at this time induces a stress reaction that proves to be extremely threatening to the immature system. This constant state of stress translates into fear, which surfaces as hyperactivity, defiance, anger, and poor peer relations, among others behavioral characteristics.

This continues to escalate throughout the school years until, in such an environment; the child with a cognitive age of twelve is interacting from an emotional perspective anywhere from two to maybe six years of age. This is all dependent on the environment in which he is currently being nurtured and guided in his development. Over time, this lack of ability to feel calm within the school environment will begin to take its toll on all involved, including parents, teachers, and peers, but most of all, the student himself. At this point the thought of school becomes a stress-provoking event because his parents are stressed about receiving calls everyday and negative reports, the teachers are frustrated with this immature child, and the other peers have begun bullying the child because he responds in highly inappropriate ways to what is considered typical childhood teasing. The child, however, is responding exactly the way a child of his emotional age would respond; with extreme ranges of sadness, anger, and threatening behavior. In the classroom, the perceived threatening environment causes the child to react in fear. He may become violent or highly oppositional, completely resistant to following through on any manner of request.

Education and the Child of Trauma

Working as a Team for Development

The school and parents must work together to provide the environment most conducive for the child. In my work with students that present such an overwhelming discrepancy between emotional and cognitive age, a number of changes must be initiated.

First, it must be stated that emotional growth and development are not the primary motives of the educational system. The primary motive is education. Education is highly applicable to cognitive ability, but it is not conducive to emotional learning. Emotional learning must initiate within the family system; however, it can be greatly supported and enhanced by the school system, and vice versa. Second, the family is the center of our educational and emotional development, so with proper support and encouragement from the family system, the student will be better prepared to receive the expertise offered from the educational system.

Specific recommendations have been established to assist children with a trauma history in receiving the most appropriate environment conducive to stimulating their emotional development within the capabilities of the school and family. It must be recognized that without the development of the emotional regulatory ability, most school experiences for this child will be a negative. The following are suggestions for helping the child with a trauma history to have more success within the educational learning environment:

• **Modified School Schedule:** A modified school schedule may be presented to assist the child in receiving the highest level of educational exposure within the range of his emotional tolerance. This schedule would have the child attending school on a half-day schedule. Areas such as homework and class projects would be best completed in the home environment with the parent's presence. The proposed, modified schedule will keep stressors at a minimum, enabling the child to utilize the cognitive skill capacities he demonstrates during less stressful times. It is not uncommon for a child with a trauma history to demonstrate high intelligence when the environment is one of calm interaction and allows the child to fully access his cognitive ability.

• **Reduced Peer Interaction:** Reduced peer interaction may perhaps prove to be the most beneficial modification to aid this child in his developmental improvement. Often times, a child with a trauma history will be the target of bullying or taunting. Being relieved of an environment in which emotional bullying can be at its worst, will allow this child to function in the least restrictive environment, eliminating the stress stemming from the emotions of fear, shame, and anger. Peer contact is defined in the school environment as lunchtime, physical education, recess, etc.

• **Daily, Consistent, One-on-One Mentoring:** A one-to-one mentor will provide the child with a secure figure within which he can develop a sense of trust, security and dependence in the absence of the parent. Independence for this child is counter-productive. Developing a relationship with a mentor can create an environment for corrective emotional experiences with a trusted figure outside of the primary caregiver.

• **Secure, Low-Stimulus Environment:** A low-stimulus environment will maintain that the child is in an environment of minimal stressors. Due to the sensitive nature of this child's Stress Response System, the lower the external stimulus the more opportunity the child has to maintain a state of regulation, hence, calm. This state of neurophysiological functioning is pertinent to the success of this child in the formal educational environment.

• **High Structure:** Structure with minimal change provides the child an opportunity to acclimate to the expectations of the coming school day and to maintain the resonance and regulation gained throughout the previous evening and night's rest cycle.

• **Interactive Communication:** The one-to-one mentor must be pro-active in a) using a tone of voice that is firm yet non-threatening, b) ensuring the understanding of communication through requesting and gaining eye contact, and c) providing the child with non-threatening physical expressions such as hugs, pats, head rubs, etc. These seemingly standard actions are oftentimes underrated when working with children. These gestures further enable the child to develop trust and dependence, which will be pertinent factors in situations of stress.

• **Counseling Sessions within the Educational Setting:** Weekly sessions will allow all involved to monitor progress, set goals, and assist the child in developing relaxation techniques and appropriate methods of emotional expression.

• **Daily Telephone Contact from the Parent:** Daily telephone contact between the parent and child will maximize the child's ability to maintain regulatory functioning throughout the school day. Contact with the primary caregiver will provide the child with an added sense of security while in the educational environment. This contact may be on a routine schedule or initiated as needed by the child. Also, daily contact between the one-on-one mentor and the parent will provide a rapport between the school and the home, which will greatly improve collaboration and communication.

In Summary

Though it may appear to the untrained eye that such changes may further jeopardize the educational growth of this student, this assumption could not be further from the need for developmental appropriateness. The modification to this child's current educational exposure will assist greatly in his ability to develop the skills necessary to better utilize his cognitive abilities when placed in emotionally stressful situations. As this child continues to function in the least restrictive environment created for maintained emotional regulation, his cognitive ability will be allowed to function without the constant interference of stress overload. As the time between highly stressful events becomes longer his brain will be allotted an opportunity for development.

This aspect of development within the limbic system is ultimately responsible for stress regulation and the effective use of cognitive ability. Determining such progress can be assessed incrementally and over time, through much the same means as with other children. Such measure might include reporting by those directly involved in the student's activities, the assessment of the completion of required educational tasks, and occasional comparison testing in such unstructured tasks as handwriting.

It may possibly be feasible to begin to reintroduce this student into the full-time environment within a six-month time frame, with close monitoring. When this time nears, it is highly recommended that an IEP meeting be held to determine appropriate degrees of introduction and the assurance that consistent monitoring will take place.

School time experiences for all children are valuable learning opportunities. Unfortunately for children with trauma histories, school can also become a very negative experience that only serves to keep them in their current state of arrested emotional development. Take the time to assess the history of this child and make the appropriate modifications to his school learning experience.

Common Questions and Answers:

The Stress Model

Family-Centered Regulatory Therapy

Family-Centered Regulatory Parenting

Family-Centered Intensive Therapy

B. Bryan Post, PhD, LCSW

Common Questions and Answers

I am often asked questions about my work with families and the particular approaches I have developed called Family-Centered Regulatory Parenting and Intensive Family-Centered Regulatory Therapy. Following are some of the most common questions I am asked when I lecture on this subject.

Q: What is your area of specialization?

A: I specialize in the treatment of behavioral and emotional disorders demonstrated by children and families. Primarily, this involves families with children that act out with severe behaviors. Normally, these behaviors range from lying, stealing, and manipulating, to setting fires and hurting others. Often times these children are diagnosed with Reactive Attachment Disorder; however, they may also have been diagnosed as Oppositional-Defiant, Bi-Polar, ADHD, or even Post-Traumatic Stress Disorder. I place heavy emphasis on the family because this is the center of the healing environment for the child, and also because the family is generally reacting to an enormous amount of stress as well.

Q: Is there a specific age that you work with?

A: Obviously, due to the neurological implications, the younger the child the better. However, I have worked with all ages of children and have had the same amount of success with teens as with younger children.

Q: How can I know for sure whether my family could benefit from Intensive Family-Centered Regulatory Therapy?

A: Unfortunately, there is no way to know for sure which particular therapy will benefit your family. It would be unethical of me to make that kind of claim. What I will say, however, is that I believe, of all the different types of therapy available, mine will offer your family the greatest opportunity for healing, in the most efficient period of time. Most families I have worked with have been through years of other therapies and have spent countless dollars. I believe that I have identified the root cause to dysfunctional behavior. When my concepts are applied correctly and consistently, healing can begin in a very short period of time. I strongly believe that the only time this therapy fails a family is when the parents become resistant to the healing path. As you may know, healing does not come easily. I do not work miracles. I work hard and the families I work with must work even harder to experience true healing.

Q: Do you also use traditional therapy methods? How many families have you worked with using Family-Centered Regulatory Therapy?

A: I started as a traditional therapist. I have worked with a couple of hundred families altogether. I can honestly say that Family-Centered Regulatory Therapy has come at the expense of my spending a lot of time providing traditional therapy to families, and not being able to help them find true healing until I discovered the Stress Model. Since conceptualizing The Stress Model, I have seen a great deal of healing take place.

Q: Were there any families that were unsuccessful?

A: I believe that only a family can determine their own success or failure. If I fail with a family it's because I failed to communicate effectively to them the soul of the message that all behavior arises from the neurophysiological state of stress, and the emotion of fear, and it is through the fear that we can heal the hurt and diminish the behavior.

Q: What is the difference between your Intensive Family-Centered Regulatory Therapy and some of the other intensive programs offered across the country?

A: There is great variety in the approaches used in the various different intensive therapy programs. I choose to work in the family's

Common Questions and Answers

home rather than having them travel to me. My program lasts six months. Over the last couple of years I have been able to determine that it takes exactly six months of follow through for a family to move effectively into the path of healing. In this manner I have created a program to maintain my involvement throughout that phase. I place more emphasis on the whole family dynamics, and specifically, the parental dyad; while most approaches place their emphasis on the child and his behavior. My parenting recommendations for after the intensive will also be quite different from what you will find in other programs. The biggest difference is probably in my theoretical foundation, which you can learn about in my writings on The Stress Model. There is also a significant difference in the level of follow-up support I provide after the intensive, which I feel is very important.

Q: How long does the intensive last? Will we need to take time off work or set aside a certain amount of time after the intensive to adjust to this new approach to parenting?

A: The entire program lasts six months. An average initial intensive phase lasts three days. 60-90 days later, I will make a return follow-up visit. This will allow the family time to implement the newly learned responses and strategies, in addition to processing what areas need to be addressed further. Throughout the rest of the time we will have constant phone and e-mail contact. Everyone will need to be home for the entire duration of the initial intensive phase and for my return follow-up visit. You may go on with life as usual afterward. I am not simply providing therapy, like your traditional once per week therapy. I am providing you with a way of life. I will point out certain areas for you to be aware of in your daily life and several changes to make in your routine. I will also give you recommendations to assist in the school process.

Q: Why do you do your work in the family's home rather than in your office?

A: One day I was reading a book about the great hypnotist and psychiatrist, Milton Erickson, and it explained that he used to make home visits and expressed how well his clients responded. I thought that was the greatest thing - to actually confront the hurt of families in their own home. How much more powerful could that be! Families are welcome to come to my office if they choose, but I prefer to go to their homes. It is less stressful and more cost-effective for the family, and it allows me to get a closer look at the "real" family.

Q: Do you work with the extended family or just with the immediate family?

A: I prefer to work only with the immediate family. The inclusion of the adult children is also very beneficial as well.

Q: I understand that my stress affects my child, but you talk so much about the parents dysregulation, that it almost sounds like I am the cause of my child's problems, rather than the problems being caused by the trauma during the child's early life. Am I misunderstanding this?

A: It is correct that the cause of the dysregulation stems from the early trauma; however, the maintenance of regulation within the child's system is directly related to the state of the parents. Simply having a child like this in their home causes the parents a great deal of stress. If the parents remain dysregulated, then the child fails to receive a healing environment. Therefore, the regulation of the parents must be addressed first, because this is the primary source of the child's healing, both in biological and adoptive situations.

Q: You stress the importance of working with the parents first. What if my spouse and I don't have any significant issues to deal with? Is this the wrong therapy for us?

A: I will always focus on the family as a whole, starting with the parents. The less parental issues there are, the more solid the foundation, and the more opportunity I have to focus on the child's past trauma and current stressors. I will certainly explore every area your family has to offer, and we can also spend time on core parenting and day-to-day issues. I feel that every family can benefit from my work, even those that are not encountering any problems at all. The

Common Questions and Answers

understanding that you will receive can be of use in all areas of life, and you may be able to help others in need.

Q: Using "containment" in therapy sounds both difficult and invasive. It seems much more suitable to working with a younger child. I've heard you even work with adults using "containment." It sounds especially awkward between adults. Is it difficult at first? Does it get easier? How do most people respond to it?

A: The only time I recommend and utilize containment is during the actual initial intensive phase. I believe containment should only be done in the context of the family environment and under the immediate supervision of the therapist. I do not instruct or encourage families to do holdings at home without their therapist. Containment or holding should never be controlling, punitive, aggressive, confrontational or harsh. One cannot overcome fear through force, but only through love. In this manner, all containment done in therapy is loving, encouraging, understanding, and accepting, period. In fact, in my most recent work I have begun to redefine containment, or holding, in the manner in which I conduct it as a 'Dyadic Supportive Environment.' I believe this is more in line with the work I now do. I have experienced and practiced the gamut of treatment styles and it has taken much of my own inner work and acknowledgement as well as a dedication to healing and peace, for me to make it back to this perspective. The only holding done in a family should be loving holding. If a parent is unable to calm their child without touching them, then they should not lay hands upon him. It is much easier for holding to be forced upon a child because that buys into both the therapist's and parent's own fear about not being in control. The only time we seek to control is when we are afraid. Children should not be forced into holding. When a child does not feel threatened then he or she will never resist the loving arms of a parent.

Q: Besides extreme rage, my child struggles with learning disabilities and has trouble getting along with friends. Can your therapy help with these or other problems as well?

A: Fear is the primary emotion. What we mistake as rage or anger is in fact at the root only fear. Nevertheless, for this question I will refer you back to the treatment protocol where I talk about the orbitofrontal cortex. This is the center of our learning and emotional-social development. This center is also highly affected by stress, so certainly when the stress is brought within regulation, all of the other areas will begin to improve. I believe that it is a developmentally corrective approach for children, and even for adults in some cases, if they remain open to the work. Primarily, because it addresses stress directly, the orbitofrontal cortex is most affected by stress. The orbitofrontal cortex is also the one area of the brain that remains open to change throughout the life span. Now that is exciting!

Q: What if my child is incorrectly diagnosed with Reactive Attachment Disorder (RAD)? What if my child actually has Post Traumatic Stress Disorder, Oppositional Defiant Disorder, Conduct Disorder, Bipolar Disorder or Attention Deficit Disorder? Will the intensive be rendered useless to these or other types of brain dysfunction? Do I need to be sure of my child's RAD diagnosis before attempting an intensive?

A: I treat families, not labels. It is not necessary to have a diagnosis of RAD. I work with families with various types of behavioral concerns. The most confusing aspect of mental health when it comes to parents, is the misinformation that they are given from misinformed, often times misled, physicians. It has never been proven that Bipolar, ADHD, or any of the other disorders are a genetic condition. Your child is being given a label for a behavior.

Q: How does medication affect your type of therapy? Would it be best if my child were off all medications during the intensive?

A: It is not necessary to take your child off any medication prior to the intensive; however, it would greatly enhance the process by not having your child's natural expressions arrested by medication. I am not an advocate of psychotropic medication for children at any time. I know that healing can take place without medication. Most of the children I work with have had numerous medication changes. This merely proves that the brain is remarkably powerful, and over an extended period of time, medication is rendered power-

Common Questions and Answers

less over the effects of the brain. During the intensive phase I will be accessing deeper brain release patterns, which are far more significant than the level that the medication is affecting. Certainly, on the second day, it will not be necessary for your child to receive the medications. Following the intensive, I recommend a medication evaluation by the child's psychiatrist. By this time, I believe the family is generally ready to conquer their problems without the use of psychotropic medications. Most families feel confident enough to do this after the intensive.

Q: My hope is that my child can be off all medications once we address his problems through your Intensive Family-Centered Regulatory Therapy and Family-Centered Regulatory Parenting. Am I being too optimistic?

A: I certainly believe that you will be able to get your child off all medications. You are not being too optimistic. Maybe everyone else has just been too pessimistic. I just tend to be realistic! All of the data on medications is so suspect and so laden by research conducted by pharmaceutical companies, that parents and physicians are just not given a clear picture. We live in a medication-driven society. I recommend reading Peter R. Breggin, M.D.'s books to gain more insight into medications and their research.

Q: I understand that you teach how to deal with stress as it occurs. What about stress that occurs when I am not with my child to address it? Will my child be able to address it on his own?

A: My entire approach and theory is ultimately geared towards your child being able to have the capacity for effective self-regulation. I have seen wonderful regulatory progress made in as little as two days, but the ongoing capacity to regulate outside of parental presence is developmental and can only be determined by where your child is at now and at what level your child is already successfully functioning. The level of functioning will increase by using Family-Centered Regulatory Parenting.

Q: Will you teach me what to do if my child misbehaves in

88

public?

A: I will show you two things – how to avoid misbehavior in public and what to do if it arises. You will also understand the causes of misbehavior and why it arises in public. A discipline program in the home does not assure success in public, but a stressed-out child at home will surely guarantee a misbehaving child in public.

Q: What kind of follow-up support will we need after the intensive and how will that be provided?

A: I take my work very seriously and have a strong desire to see each family succeed in healing; therefore, I will provide a sufficient amount of follow-up e-mails and phone consults between the times of each visit. I will make a complete assessment during my time with your family and if I feel weekly follow-up therapy is necessary, I will work with your local therapist to provide this support.

Q: What changes should we expect to see immediately after the intensive, and then what gradual changes after that, and in what time frame?

A: Immediately, you will see your child in a different light. No longer will he seem so distant and rejecting, but he will be more open to you and affectionate. The outbursts should more than likely dissipate entirely during the first 30 days. After about thirty days it would depend on your follow-through as parents. If you continue to address his stress when it appears in his behavior, you will rarely, if ever, see another outburst. Instead, you will see signs of frustration and hear statements of feelings. You will feel stronger as a parent and more empowered to help your child express his emotions. You and your spouse will experience closeness on a level that has not been felt in a long time, and the same will be true for other family members. Most of this should be present by the last day of the intensive. I work hard to establish a foundation for the parents to build on. I will make several recommendations to you concerning your child. I would predict that in six months you would be in a very good place as a family, and in a year you will be well into the healing

Common Questions and Answers

process. It is not miracle work. Sometimes it seems like it because it is so powerful, but it is very hard work and requires follow-through and support. I will actively provide the support.

Final Word: The bottom line is that there are hundreds of different approaches to treating emotional and behavioral disruptions. On average the families I have worked with have tried other forms of therapy for an average of eight years before seeking out my service. Also, they have spent sometimes $20,000 or more. I encourage you to seek out the treatment that seems to fit your family and their needs. If and when you decide to work with me, be committed, prepared, and open to the healing process.

A New Book Coming Soon!!!

Born In Fear...
Understanding and Parenting Adopted and Foster Children.

"Both adopted and foster children have experienced trauma which not only goes unresolved, but is misunderstood by main stream society. Early trauma can create an imprint within a child's brain and body system causing a lifelong impact. It is imperative that we begin expanding our awareness of behavior by taking a deeper look into its origin. Rather than continually pruning back the leaves, it is time to search nearer to the roots. I invite you to attend this learning experience as we explore the pathways from hurt to healing."

– Dr. B. Bryan Post

RAD, ADHD, PTSD, Depression and Bi-Polar...all conditions affecting adopted and foster children...all treatable with Dr. Post's methods.

What You Will Learn:

- Neuroscientific Findings Destined to Change Mental Health Treatment of Children and Families
- The Therapeutic Environment: Helping Children Heal Without Therapy
- Understand the Impact of Trauma on Early Brain Development
- Learn Why Cognitive-Based Treatment Approaches Do Not Stand the Test of Time Against Trauma
- Learn Effective Treatment and Parenting Techniques for Immediate and Dramatic Change
- Teaching Tools for Educational Success

About the Author

B. Bryan Post is an Internationally recognized specialist in the treatment of trauma in children and families. An adopted child himself, Dr. Post has made it his primary work to speak to parents and professionals from a perspective of true-life examples, based on his own life and those of the countless families he has successfully treated. Utilizing his insight and knowledge, Dr. Post has developed The Stress Model Theory and Family-Centered Regulatory Therapy as an effective means for helping families reach dramatic change in short periods of time and move into a place of healing. Dr. Post has lectured and provided expert consultation regarding adoption, trauma, attachment and bonding throughout the United States, Canada and Australia.

Dr. Post is a Licensed Clinical Social Worker in the state of Oklahoma and is registered to practice within various other states. His nationally focused private practice is based in Oklahoma, where he resides with his family.

Dr. Post is available to conduct trainings, provide consultation and in-home therapeutic services. For more information visit:
www.postinstitute.com
or call 866-848-POST

Don't forget to sign-up for free articles and a monthly e-newsletter at www.postinstitute.com